D0816726

Andrew Marvell

The Garden

Officially Withdrawn

Edited by
Thomas O. Calhoun
University of Delaware

John M. Potter
Hunter College of CUNY

The Merrill Literary Casebook Series
Edward P. J. Corbett, Editor

Charles E. Merrill Publishing Company
A Bell & Howell Company
Columbus, Ohio

Copyright © 1970 by CHARLES E. MERRILL PUBLISHING COM-
PANY, Columbus, Ohio. All rights reserved. No part of this
book may be reproduced in any form, electronic or me-
chanical, including photocopy, recording, or any informa-
tion storage and retrieval system without permission in
writing from the publisher.

ISBN: 0-675-09301-5

Library of Congress Catalog Number: 73-126736

1 2 3 4 5 6 7 8 9 10—76 75 74 73 72 71 70

Printed in the United States of America

500173

Foreword

The Charles E. Merrill Literary Casebook Series deals with short literary works, arbitrarily defined here as "works which can be easily read in a single sitting." Accordingly, the series will concentrate on poems, short stories, brief dramas, and literary essays. These casebooks are designed to be used in literature courses or in practical criticism courses where the instructor wants to expose his students to an extensive and intensive study of a single, short work or in composition courses where the instructor wants to expose his students to the discipline of writing a research paper on a literary text.

All of the casebooks in the series follow this format: (1) foreword; (2) the author's introduction; (3) the text of the literary work; (4) a number of critical articles on the literary work; (5) suggested topics for short papers on the literary work; (6) suggested topics for long (10-15 pages) papers on the literary work; (7) a selective bibliography of additional readings on the literary work; (8) general instructions for the writing of a research paper. Some of the casebooks, especially those dealing with poetry, may carry an additional section, which contains such features as variant versions of the work, a closely related literary work, comments by the author and his contemporaries on the work.

So that students might simulate first-hand research in library copies of books and bound periodicals, each of the critical articles carries full bibliographical information at the bottom of the first page of the article, and the text of the article carries the actual page-numbers of the original source. A notation like /131/ after a word in the text indicates that *after* that word in the original source the article went over to page 131. All of the text between that number and the next number, /132/, can be taken as occurring on page 131 of the original source.

Edward P.J. Corbett
General Editor

iii

Contents

Introduction   1

Hortus by Andrew Marvell   11

The Garden by Andrew Marvell   15

William Empson, *Marvell's Garden*   18

Ruth Wallerstein, *Marvell and the Various Light*   25

Milton Klonsky, *A Guide Through the Garden*   41

Frank Kermode, *The Argument of Marvell's "Garden"*   52

Pierre Legouis, *Marvell and the New Critics*   68

Maren-Sofie Røstvig, *Andrew Marvell's
    "The Garden": A Hermetic Poem*   75

Stanley N. Stewart, *Marvell and "The Garden Enclosed"*   92

J. B. Leishman, *The Garden*   118

Suggestions for Papers   134

Additional Readings   137

General Instructions For A Research Paper   139

Introduction

Andrew Marvell, Jr. was born in March, 1621. His father was a preacher, a graduate of the puritan Emmanuel College, an advocate of Calvinism, and probably a supporter of Parliament over the King. The young Marvell attended Hull Grammar School near the Holy Trinity Church where his father was lecturer. The elder Marvell was also Master of the Charterhouse (Almshouse) at Hull, and this position provided the family with a rural home and gardens.

Marvell was drilled in the essentials of composition at Hull. During the seventeenth century, education consisted chiefly of studying classical languages, particularly Latin. The object was for the student to be able to read, write, and often speak Latin fluently. Part of the daily work was to translate Latin poetry into English and vice versa. Thus a student had a great deal of practice in writing Latin verses, and many English poets wrote their own poems in Latin. John Milton, Marvell's friend and political mentor, wrote first in Latin, and had to make a conscious choice between the universality of Latin and the greater expressiveness of English for his most important poems. But when he wished to write something that future ages would not willingly let die, he chose English because "by certain vital signs it had, it was likely to live."

When he was twelve years old, Andrew entered Trinity College, Cambridge, as a scholarship student. His first published poem, "A Parody for King Charles," appeared in a 1637 Cambridge volume dedicated to Princess Anne. This is a Latin poem, based on a classical model. The technique Marvell used is called *parodia*, a form of literary imitation that may be compared to writing a descant upon a given melody. Marvell's poem in the Cambridge volume follows Horace's Ode I. ii, point by point, but he allowed himself the freedom to make variations in diction, subject, and implication where he chose.

Marvell remained at Cambridge until he was twenty, but he published no more poetry there. In 1638 his mother died, and his father remarried six months later. In 1639 Marvell converted to Catholicism

1

and ran away from Cambridge, perhaps seeking the dangerous, austere, and intellectually rigorous life of a Jesuit. His father found him in a bookstore, "rescued" him, and sent him back to school—so the story goes. In 1640 Marvell's father drowned. The poet left Trinity College in 1641, without finishing his Master of Arts degree, and in the following year the English Civil War began in earnest. While England saw the beginnings of a decade which would end in public approval of regicide, Marvell was touring continental Europe. He stayed in Holland, France, Italy, and Spain. According to John Milton, he learned the languages of these countries while on tour. Why Marvell left England, and how this trip was financed, are not known. Aside from a meeting with Richard Flecknoe which resulted in an unpublished satire, the poet's European activities are also unknown. But Marvell's insular background, which may have dictated his characteristic quietness in company, gained a new, cosmopolitan dimension by this experience.

In 1646 or thereabouts Marvell returned to England. He came to London, found a place in the Royalist, "cavalier" society there, and wrote some occasional and complimentary poetry. One poem appears in the elegaic collection *Lachrymae Musarum*, 1648; another poem prefaces Richard Lovelace's *Lucasta*, 1649. Complimentary poetry, usually not taken too seriously, is a type of verse written to congratulate a friend on his personal characteristics or achievements. Poetic compliments were nearly always added as prefatory matter to books published in the seventeenth century, just as selections from favorable critical reviews are often printed on book-jackets today. Occasional poetry was written to celebrate special events, such as births and deaths in the Royal family, and sometimes to describe and celebrate certain places such as houses and estates.

The evidence of these few poems does not establish that Marvell's attachment to the "cavalier" movement was necessarily intimate. Marvell's literary associates were mostly Royalists, but he did not fully sympathize with their cause. Nor was he an outright Parliamentarian and supporter of Cromwell, as his father probably would have been had he lived to see the execution of King Charles I.

Oliver Cromwell succeeded Thomas, Third Baron Fairfax, as Commander of the Parliamentary Armies in 1650. Fairfax resigned probably because he could not condone the murder of the King. He retired to his country estates, preferring Nun Appleton House in Yorkshire to several others, and in 1651 hired Andrew Marvell as a tutor for his twelve-year-old daughter Mary. During Marvell's brief stay with the Fairfax family, from 1651 until 1653, most of his lyric poems, including "The Garden," were probably written. So we shall sketch the remaining details of the poet's life briefly and then return to Nun Appleton House and 1651.

In 1653 John Milton, Latin Secretary to the Parliamentary government, recommended that his friend Andrew Marvell be appointed assistant secretary. This arrangement did not come about until 1657. In the meantime, Marvell was at Eton serving as a tutor for John Dutton, a young protégé of Oliver Cromwell. After working with Milton for two years, Marvell became a member of Parliament for Hull. He held this position from 1659 until his death in 1678. During this last phase of his life Marvell wrote political satires and controversial prose pamphlets—notably *The Rehearsal Transpos'd*. Unlike Milton, whose personal and political character did not survive the Restoration, Marvell was able to satirize public figures, ministers, and even the King without harming his reputation as a responsible member of the government.

We know little about Marvell's private life. He never married. John Aubrey, the poet's first biographer, suggests that "he kept bottles of wine at his lodgeing, and many times he would drinke liberally by himself to refresh his spirits, and exalt his Muse." Marvell died in 1678, and three years later his *Miscellaneous Poems* were published by a woman, Mary Marvell, who claimed to be his widow.

We can assume that Marvell's two-year term at the estates of General Fairfax was a time of physical leisure and intellectual stimulation. His job as tutor couldn't have been too demanding. Though Marvell describes Mary as an alert and pleasant girl, she was never much of a scholar. There was ample time to read and write, and, happily, Thomas Fairfax was a book collector as well as an amateur poet and translator. His library was a good one. As you will observe in the critical essays which follow in this book, Fairfax's activities as a poet and translator are considered an important influence on Marvell's "The Garden." Ruth Wallerstein talks of the "Yorkshire estate" in her essay and compares "The Garden" with the poetry of one of Fairfax's favorite writers, the French libertine Saint-Amant. Frank Kermode begins his essay by dismissing the Yorkshire influence as erroneous, since "The Garden" cannot be dated precisely, but he continues to argue the important generic influence of poems like Saint-Amant's "Solitude" which, he reminds us, Fairfax translated. Maren-Sofie Røstvig's argument is based on the fact that Fairfax translated part of a French commentary on the Hermetic *Pimander*. Stanley Stewart accepts Professor Røstvig's suggestion that Fairfax and Marvell were probably working together, but he considers Fair-

fax's metrical version of the "Songe of Salomon" as the important
influence on "The Garden."

Considering that the most likely variations on the idea of Fairfax's
contribution to Marvell's poem have been explored, one might choose
another line of analysis and study the inter-relations among the
poems Marvell wrote during his Yorkshire retreat. Most critics and
editors will agree that "Upon the Hill and Grove at Bill-borow" and
"Upon Appleton House" were written between 1651 and 1653. They
are both addressed to Fairfax, and each describes a Fairfax estate.
Other probable candidates for this period include the four mower
poems—"Damon the Mower," "The Mower to the Glo-Worms," "The
Mower Against Gardens," and "The Mower's Song"—"On a Drop of
Dew" with its Latin version "Ros," and, of course, "The Garden" with
its Latin companion "Hortus."

Both "Hortus" and "The Garden" are odes. Consideration of the
poems in terms of this basic form is important, because the concept
of genre was vital to a poet of the seventeenth century such as
Marvell. He held that all poems could be ordered in certain specific
classes. These generic classes, the pastoral, the ode, the epigram and
the elegy for example, were established by the Greeks. The generic
type of a poem is historically given, then, and not reasoned or in-
vented by the poet himself. Marvell considered his poems not as
isolated events but as parts of an historic continuity.

The term ode (ᾠδή), which comes from ἀείδειν, to sing, was adopted
by the Renaissance humanists for the more general term *carmen*,
which Horace had applied to his odes. There have been several
studies on the development of the ode as a modern form.[1] From
these, one must conclude that a purely formal definition of the genre
cannot be realized. No meter or formal requirement will fit all odes.
The closest one can come to a definition is to say that the ode is a
lyric of medium length which treats a subject more seriously than
do the shorter lyrics (such as songs, sonnets, etc.). The effect is one
of lyric thoughtfulness.

Originally the word *ode* was used to designate a poem written in
the manner of Pindar, Anacreon, or Horace. Although Pindar and the
(misconceived) "irregular" odes were the most influential models
for poets of the mid-seventeenth century, both "Hortus" and "The
Garden" are in the manner of Horace. It is helpful then to summarize
briefly the most significant characteristics of the Horatian ode. This

---

[1] Cf. Carol Maddison, *Apollo and the Nine* (London: Routledge and Kegan
Paul,1960) ; Robert Shafer, *The English Ode to 1660* (Princeton: University Press,
1918) ; George N. Shuster, *The English Ode from Milton to Keats* (New York:
Columbia University Press, 1940).

ode develops through contrast; the structure is essentially antithet-
ical. There is a progression of significance rather than a sense of
completion or resolution. Steele Commager explains this development
in terms of the imagery of one of the odes: "The Ode progresses
through these antithetical similes and metaphors, and its logic lies in
terms of the various tensions it so maintains." In his introduction to
the Cleopatra Ode he states this idea again in broader terms:

> Most obvious is Horace's fondness for an antithetical arrangement of
> themes and ideas, and we can watch the verbal contrasts and repetitions
> that he so often exploits in individual stanzas develop into an archi-
> tectural control for whole poems.[2]

These antitheses create the tone as well as the structure of the odes.
Horace treats each subject with a proper mixture of sobriety and
levity; he has a sense of self-irony about even the most serious of
subjects. But, as Eduard Fraenkel remarks in his discussion of *Integer
vitae*, "from the easy grace of the ode and the mock-solemnity in
some of its expressions it does not follow that there is no deeper
feeling behind it."[3] In Horace we are concerned with more than a
simple matter of contrasts or antithetical images; often the different
sections of the poem stand in a kind of complementary contrast. This
kind of contrast may lead to a fragmented reading of a poem. If a
reader insists too strongly that the contrasting sections are competing,
as in an argument, one section is often thought to contain the "real
meaning" of the poem, and the total poem is ignored or distorted.
However, properly perceived, the organization through completing
contrasts results in the perfect poise of urbanity and feeling that
readers have seen as the distinctive quality which links Horace and
Marvell.

"Hortus," the Latin version of "The Garden," has been included
in this book chiefly as a point of comparison and contrast to the
English "Garden." It is, however, an interesting poem in its own
right. John Aubrey records an estimation of Marvell's Latin poetry:

> He was a great master of the Latin tongue; an excellent poet in Latin or
> English: for Latin verses there was no man could come into competi-
> tion with him.

The whole body of Marvell's Latin poetry comprises only sixteen
poems, nine of which are short epigrams; all are in elegiacs, except

---

2 Steele Commager, *The Odes of Horace* (New Haven, 1962), pp. 65, 88.
3 Eduard Fraenkel, *Horace* (Oxford, 1957), p. 187.

"Hortus," "Upon an Eunuch," and the translation from Brebeuf, which are in hexameters, and the Parody to King Charles, which reproduces the sapphics of Horace's original. Despite the small amount of Marvell's Latin poetry and its lack of metrical originality, it was evidently admired by his contemporaries.

As it stands, "Hortus" is a conventional denial of ambition and power in favor of the quiet private life of a country gentleman. As such it is more in the tradition of Ben Jonson and his tribe than the metaphysical tradition of Donne. It shares with poems like Jonson's "To Penshurst" the peculiar adaptation of lighter Roman themes to an English setting. The poem is built on a very simple set of contrasts: in the first part, between the daily activity of men, the labor, complexity and noise, and the peace, simplicity, and silence of contemplation; in the second part, between the passionate activity of love and the calm reflection (in Apollo and Pan) of art. The conclusion celebrates the poet's choice of contemplation over action by envisioning the one active principle—time—which cannot be denied, the one that relates all the labors of men as subject to the symbols of quiet contemplation, so that even the busy bee measures his *thoughts* by "sundial thyme."

Marvell's Latin style, like his English, presents the reader with a smooth elegant surface which conceals depths of complexity. He uses metaphyhical puns which link two antithetical ideas. His puns are of two types: the Latin puns and the macaronic (i.e., English and Latin) puns. The pun on *libro* is an example of a Latin pun.

> *Nulla Neaera, Chloe, Faustina, Corynna, legetur:*
> *In proprio sed quaeque libro signabitur Arbos.*
> *O charae Platanus, Cyparissus, Populus, Ulmus!*

> (No Neaera, Chloe, Faustina, Corynna would be read there,
> but each tree will be printed on its own bark/book.
> O precious Plane, Cypress, Poplar, Elm!)

The play on "bark"/"book" is the connecting link between the ladies of the previous line, three of whom are mistresses in the elegiac poets and hence bookish, with the trees of the following lines. In this way the metaphysical audacity of substituting trees for ladies is created in the pun. Tonally it enforces the playful attitude of the passage; the play on "bark"/"book" signals the mock heroic of *O charae Platanus* just as it reflects the mock horror of *Nulla*. In this way the pun at once creates image and tone.

Far more important than the Latin puns are the macaronic puns, that is, puns where the play is between an English and a Latin meaning. They connect the English poet with his Latin style, and make it a neo-Latin rather than classical style. The macaronic pun on thyme (1. 56) which suggests the English time and perhaps even the Greek θυμός, soul, expresses, in its connection of thyme/time, the central balance of the poem. A harmonization of activity and growth, rest and contemplation, gives this resolution a sense of completeness.

Marvell's Latin style does not employ elaborate metaphors as such. Marvell has developed his own device, which may be called the "conceited allusion," to help create his characteristic complexity of tone and style. These allusions, although often classical, do not exist in the direct one-to-one relationship of the Augustan poets. Rather they have the multi-level interplay which is characteristic of a conceit. They are often used to exhibit a playful piece of wit. The balance of this wit is most apparent when Marvell uses allusions playfully, twisted so that it is half serious, half comic:

> *Nulla Neaera, Chloe, Faustina, Corynna, legetur:*
> (No Neaera, Chloe, Faustina, Corynna would be found there;)

Here the name of Faustina, the Roman empress famous for her profligacy, rests coyly among the standard pastoral nymphs. More significantly, the most famous love stories of myth are given a Marvellian twist. That is, they are modified to suit his poetic purpose:

> *Et licet experti toties Nymphaeque Deasque,*
> *Arbore nunc melius potiuntur quisque cupita.*
>
> (And although he is allowed to put the nymphs and
> goddesses to the test as often as he will, each one
> now prefers to realize his desires in a tree.)

Jupiter loves the oak, Mars the ash, Apollo the laurel, and Pan a reed. The theme, a denial of sexual love in favor of Epicurean contemplation, is serious; the method of expression, the gods seducing (*pellice*) trees, is decidedly playful. The conceited nature of these allusions adds much to the complexity of Marvell's Latin poems.

The style of the English poem is more compressed than the Latin, and this fact has led most critics to suggest that "Hortus" was written before "The Garden." Only one, Carl E. Bain, suggests that the English version was first.[4] Mr. Margoliouth, the editor of the text used in this book, says most sensibly that, as there is no proof, one cannot know: "It may be simplest to regard these poems as experi-

---

[4] Carl E. Bain, "The Latin Poetry of Andrew Marvell," *Philological Quarterly*, XXXVIII (1959), 436-49.

ments on the same themes, made at about the same time, in Latin and English."[5]

The main difference between the two poems is of course the *Desunt Multa,* meaning "much is missing," which an early editor has noted. The comment is an understatement even for an editor. Although "Hortus," as we have seen, stands very well on its own, it is the four stanzas (5, 6, 7 and 8) missing from "Hortus" which remove "The Garden" so completely from the tradition of conventional Jonsonian classicism and introduce the bewildering multiplicity of references— Christian, Hermetic, and Neo-Platonic—which has fascinated readers and critics alike. It is significant, particularly in view of the anti- thetical structure of this kind of ode, that most critics confine their comments largely to the stanzas which do not appear in the Latin.

"The Garden," like the fat man Falstaff, is important not only for its own wit but the wit it has caused in others. A short look at the contents and bibliography of this handbook will convince the reader that most of the major modern critics from Empson to Leishman have felt it necessary to say something about Marvell's "Garden." Marvell's major lyrics have in fact been something of a touchstone for the various schools of modern literary criticism. For various reasons his work has been both a test and a vindication of the new critics.

As a reading of the critics will indicate, the problem of the poem is to define exactly which of the many gardens—historical, philo- sophical, literary—Marvell is using in the poem. Is it the English country garden of Mr. Leishman, or the garden of Medieval and Renaissance Christianity of Miss Wallerstein and Mr. Stewart, or Miss Røstvig's Hermetic garden, or Plotinus' Garden of Ideas as Mr. Klonsky believes? And there are more. Certainly one association equally as obvious and important as the pastoral and Christian gardens is the Garden of Epicurus, hardly touched upon by critics. One does not need Marvell's classical education to associate gardens with Epicureanism, as the Garden was the name of Epicurus' school of thought, taken from the place where he taught, as the Stoics from the Stoa.[6]

Another consideration is the literary garden. An early example appears in Chaucer's "Knight's Tale." This reproduces the amorous

---

[5] H. M. Margoliouth, *The Poems and Letters of Andrew Marvell* (Oxford, 1963), I, 219.

[6] John M. Potter's essay on Marvell's "The Garden" and the garden of Epicurus could not be included in this collection. It will be published in *Studies in English Literature,* where it may be consulted on this point.

garden in Boccaccio's *Teseide*. In "The Knight's Tale" (11. 1955-61) the portrait of Venus's statue appears crowned with a red-rose garland, naked and white to the waist, and covered from the navel down with "waves" of green—thus concealing her most sacred charms. The statue stands in a temple and is surrounded by wall-paintings of Venus's home on Mt. Citheron "with al the gardyn and the lustynesse" (1. 1939). Earlier in the tale, the knight Arcite describes his desire to make love with the euphemism "getting some greene" (1. 1512). White and red are the respective colors of Venus and Mars, the potentially cruel "give and take" of courtly love.

Literary gardens related to Marvell's in various ways are also developed in Spenser's *Faerie Queen*. Consider then the garden of England in Shakespeare's *Richard II*, the forest and sheepcote of Arden in *As You Like It*, and of course Milton's Garden of Eden in *Paradise Lost*. The multiplicity of gardens which relate directly but not exclusively to Marvell's poem are a clear indication of this poet's unique ability to synthesize diverse literary and intellectual trends and create from them something new which is altogether his own.

Hortus*

Quisnam adeo, mortale genus, præcordia versat?
Heu Palmæ, Laurique furor, vel simplicis Herbæ!
Arbor ut indomitos ornet vix una labores;
Tempora nec foliis præcingat tota malignis.
Dum simul implexi, tranquillæ ad serta Quiætis,
Omnigeni coeunt Flores, integraque Sylva.
   Alma Quies, teneo te! & te Germana Quietis
Simplicitas! Vos ergo diu per Templa, per urbes,
Quæsivi, Regum perque alta Palatia frustra.
Sed vos Hortorum per opaca silentia longe   10
Celarant Plantæ virides, & concolor Umbra.
   O! mihi si vestros liceat violasse recessus
Erranti, lasso, & vitæ melioris anhelo,
Municipem servate novum, votoque potitum,
Frondosæ Cives optate in florea Regna.
   Me quoque, vos Musæ, &, te conscie testor Apollo,
Non Armenta juvant hominum, Circique boatus,
Mugitusve Fori; sed me Penetralia veris,
Horroresque trahunt muti, & Consortia sola.
   Virgineæ quem non suspendit Gratia formæ?   20
Quam candore Nives vincentem, Ostrumque rubore,
Vestra tamen viridis superet (me judice) Virtus.
Nec foliis certare Comæ, nec Brachia ramis,
Nec puduit truncis inscribere vulnera sacris.
   Ah quoties sævos vidi (quis credat?) Amantes
Sculpentes Dominæ potiori in cortice nomen?
Nec puduit truncis inscribere vulnera sacris.
Ast Ego, si vestras unquam temeravero stirpes,
Nulla Neæra, Chloe, Faustina, Corynna, legetur:
In proprio sed quæque libro signabitur Arbos.   30

---

*Texts of "Hortus" and "The Garden" from *The Poems and Letters of Andrew Marvell*, ed. H. M. Margoliouth, 2nd ed., I (Oxford, 1952), 48-51, by permission of The Clarendon Press, Oxford. Translation and notes by J. M. Potter.

O charæ Platanus, Cyparissus, Populus, Ulmus!
  Hic Amor, exutis crepidatus inambulat alis,
Enerves arcus & stridula tela reponens,
Invertitque faces, nec se cupit usque timeri;
Aut exporrectus jacet, indormitque pharetræ;
Non auditurus quanquam Cytherea vocarit;
Nequitias referunt nec somnia vana priores.
  Lætantur Superi, defervescente Tyranno,
Et licet experti toties Nymphasque Deasque,
Arbore nunc melius potiuntur quisque cupita.   40
Jupiter annosam, neglecta conjuge, Quercum
Deperit; haud alia doluit sic pellice Juno.
Lemniacum temerant vestigia nulla Cubile,
Nec Veneris Mavors meminit si Fraxinus adsit.
Formosæ pressit Daphnes vestigia Phœbus
Ut fieret Laurus; sed nil quæsiverat ultra.
Capripes & peteret quòd Pan Syringa fugacem,
Hoc erat ut Calamum posset reperire Sonorum.
                   Desunt multa
Nec tu, Opifex horti, grato sine carmine abibis:
Qui brevibus plantis, & læto flore, notasti   50
Crescentes horas, atque intervalla diei.
Sol ibi candidior fragrantia Signa pererrat;
Proque truci Tauro, stricto pro forcipe Cancri,
Securis violæque rosæque allabitur umbris.
Sedula quin & Apis, mellito intenta labori,
Horologo sua pensa thymo Signare videtur.
Temporis O suaves lapsus! O Otia sana!
  O Herbis dignæ numerari & Floribus Horæ!

English Translation of "Hortus"

Just why do mortals so disturb themselves? Oh, the rage for the palm, the laurel, the simple herb! One tree can scarcely adorn the incessant labors or wreathe all these heads with its scanty leaves. Meanwhile flowers of all kinds and a whole forest twine themselves into a garland of tranquil quiet.

I possess you, blessed peace, and you, simplicity, sister of peace. I sought you long and in vain, through temples, cities, exalted royal palaces. But green plants and green shade[10] concealed you far away in the dark silence of the gardens.

If only I were allowed to penetrate your recesses, I who wander, weary and panting for a better life. Save your new citizen and, granting my prayer, you "Leaf-people," elect me to the realm of flowers.

Muses and Apollo, I also declare myself of like mind with you. I take no delight in herds of men, the din of the circus, or the bellowing of the market place. Spring's inner chambers and numinous silences draw me, and that solitary communion.

Who is there that the grace of virgin beauty does not captivate?[20] Snow may excel in whiteness, oyster dye in redness, yet your green perfection would surpass these, I think. Hair cannot vie with leaves or arms with branches, nor can voices equal the tremulous whisperings.

How often I have seen savage lovers (who would believe it?) carve a mistress' name in bark, shamelessly inscribing wounds in the sacred trunks. Should I ever wound your trunks, no Neaera, Chloe, Faustina, Corynna would be found there; but each tree will be printed on its own bark.[30] O precious Plane, Cypress, Poplar, Elm!

Here Cupid, deprived of wings, walks about in sandals, unstrings his bow, puts down his whistling darts, inverts his torch, and no longer desires to be feared. He lies down, stretches out, and falls asleep over his quiver, indisposed to hear even Cytherea's call. And even foolish dreams don't restore previous wantonness.

The higher beings rejoice, for the tyrant has ceased to rage. And although he is allowed to put the nymphs and goddesses to the test as often as he will, each one now prefers to realize his desires in a tree.[40] Jupiter has neglected his wife and desperately loves the aged oak; no other paramour has caused Juno such pain. No traces defile the bed of Vulcan, and Mars forgets Venus if there's an ash available. Phoebus pursued beautiful Daphne so that she would become laurel; he sought nothing else. And whereas goat-footed Pan sought fleeing Syrinx, he did so in order to find a sonorous reed.

(Much is missing.)

Nor will you, Gardner, be left unsung. You have marked the growing hours and the intervals of days with short-lived plants and lush flowers.[50] The sun wanders fairer through those fragrant signs; bypassing the fierce Bull and the sharp claw of Cancer, it glides toward the secure shadows of violets and roses. Indeed the busy bee, intent on honeyed labour, seems to measure his thoughts by sundial thyme.

O sweet flight of time! O wholesome leisure! O hours worthy to be numbered in herbs and flowers!

Notes to "Hortus"

1. 2. The ancients gave wreaths made from various kinds of plants (herbae) in recognition of great achievement. For example, the oke generally was given for civic achievement, the bayes for poetic.

1. 29. Neaera, Chloe, Faustina, Corynna: All of these but Faustina were names of nymphs or shepherdesses in classical pastoral or elegiac poetry. Faustina was the name of two Roman empresses (mother and daughter) who died in 141 A.D. and 175 A.D. respectively; they were both known for their profligacy. The introduction of this name indicates that Marvell is not taking the elegiac love tradition very seriously. He is using it for its sexual rather than romantic associations.

1. 30. *libro:* the primary meaning is probably bark, but the sense of book is nearly as important.

1. 36. *Cytherea:* Venus.

1. 44. *Fraxinus:* Spears were commonly made from the ash.

1. 53. *Proque truci Tauro, stricto pro forcipe Cancri:* Menacing signs of the Zodiac are chosen to contrast with the harmless flowers of the garden. Notice *truci* and *stricto forcipe* in contrast to *Securis* of line 54. Taurus and Cancer are also appropriate as signs of spring and summer.—McQueen & Rockwell, *The Latin Poetry of Andrew Marvell* (Chapel Hill, 1964), p. 27.

1. 56. *thymo:* pun on time, perhaps also on θυμός (*animus*, soul).

The Garden

I

How vainly men themselves amaze
To win the Palm, the Oke, or Bayes;
And their uncessant Labours see
Crown'd from some single Herb or Tree.
Whose short and narrow verged Shade
Does prudently their Toyles upbraid;
While all Flow'rs and all Trees do close
To weave the Garlands of repose.

II

Fair quiet, have I found thee here,
And Innocence thy Sister dear!   10
Mistaken long, I sought you then
In busie Companies of Men.
Your sacred Plants, if here below,
Only among the Plants will grow.
Society is all but rude,
To this delicious Solitude.

III

No white nor red was ever seen
So am'rous as this lovely green.
Fond Lovers, cruel as their Flame,
Cut in these Trees their Mistress name.   20
Little, Alas, they know, or heed,
How far these Beauties Hers exceed!
Fair Trees! where s'eer your barkes I wound,
No Name shall but your own be found.

IV

When we have run our Passions heat,
Love hither makes his best retreat.

15

The *Gods,* that mortal Beauty chase,
Still in a Tree did end their race.
Apollo hunted *Daphne* so,
Only that She might Laurel grow.   30
And *Pan* did after *Syrinx* speed,
Not as a Nymph, but for a Reed.

V

What wond'rous Life in this I lead!
Ripe Apples drop about my head;
The Luscious Clusters of the Vine
Upon my Mouth do crush their Wine;
The Nectaren, and curious Peach,
Into my hands themselves do reach;
Stumbling on Melons, as I pass,
Insnar'd with Flow'rs, I fall on Grass.   40

VI

Mean while the Mind, from pleasure less,
Withdraws into its happiness:
The Mind, that Ocean where each kind
Does streight its own resemblance find;
Yet it creates, transcending these,
Far other Worlds, and other Seas;
Annihilating all that's made
To a green Thought in a green Shade.

VII

Here at the Fountains sliding foot,
Or at some Fruit-trees mossy root,   50
Casting the Bodies Vest aside,
My Soul into the boughs does glide:
There like a Bird it sits, and sings,
Then whets, and combs its silver Wings;
And, till prepar'd for longer flight,
Waves in its Plumes the various Light.

VIII

Such was that happy Garden-state,
While Man there walk'd without a Mate:

After a Place so pure, and sweet,
What other Help could yet be meet!   60
But 'twas beyond a Mortal's share
To wander solitary there:
Two Paradises 'twere in one
To live in Paradise alone.

IX

How well the skilful Gardner drew
Of flow'rs and herbes this Dial new;
Where from above the milder Sun
Does through a fragrant Zodiack run;
And, as it works, th' industrious Bee
Computes its time as well as we.   70
How could such sweet and wholsome Hours
Be reckon'd but with herbs and flow'rs!

William Empson

Marvell's Garden*

The chief point of the poem is to contrast and reconcile conscious
and unconscious states, intuitive and intellectual modes of apprehen-
sion; and yet that distinction is never made, perhaps could not have
been made; his thought is implied by his metaphors. There is some-
thing very Far-Eastern about this; I was set to work on the poem by
Dr. Richards' recent discussion of a philosophical argument in Men-
cius. The Oxford edition notes bring out a crucial double meaning
(so that this at least is not my own fancy) in the most analytical
statement of the poem, about the Mind—

> Annihilating all that's made
> To a green thought in a green shade.

'Either "reducing the whole material world to nothing material, *i.e.*
to a green thought," or "considering the material world as of no value
compared to a green thought"'; either contemplating everything or
shutting everything out. This combines the idea of the conscious
mind, including everything because understanding it, and that of the
unconscious animal nature, including everything because in harmony
with it. Evidently the object of such a fundamental contradiction
(seen in the etymology: turning all *ad nihil, to* nothing, and *to* a
thought) is to deny its reality; the point is not that these two are
essentially different but that they must cease to be different so far as
either is to be known. So far as he has achieved his state of ecstasy he
combines them, he is 'neither conscious nor not conscious,' like the

*Reprinted from *Some Versions of Pastoral*. London: Chatto & Windus, 1935,
pp. 119-20, 123-28, 130-32, by permission of the publisher, New Directions Pub-
lishing Corp., and the author. All rights reserved.

seventh /120/ Buddhist state of enlightenment. This gives it,
I think, to the other ambiguity, clear from the context, as to whether
the *all* considered was *made* in the mind of the author or the Creator;
to so peculiarly 'creative' a knower there is little difference between
the two. Here as usual with 'profound' remarks the strength of the
thing is to combine unusually intellectual with unusually primitive
ideas; thought about the conditions of knowledge with a magical idea
that the adept controls the external world by thought. . . . /123/
The theme of the *Garden* is a repose.

> How vainly men themselves amaze
> To win the Palm, or Oke, or Bayes;
> And their uncessant Labours see
> Crown'd from some single Herb or Tree.
> Whose short and narrow verged Shade
> Does prudently their Toyles upbraid;
> While all Flow'rs and all Trees do close
> To weave the Garlands of repose.

This first verse comes nearest to stating what seems the essential
distinction, with that between powers inherent and powers worked
out in practice, being a general and feeling one could be; in this ideal
case, so the wit of the thing claims, the power to have been a general
is already satisfied in the garden. 'Unemployment' is too painful and
normal even in the fullest life for such a theme to be trivial. But self-
knowledge is possible in such a state so far as the unruly impulses are
digested, ordered, made transparent, not by their being known, at the
time, as unruly. Consciousness no longer makes an important /124/
distinction; the impulses, since they must be balanced already,
neither need it to put them right nor are put wrong by the way it
forces across their boundaries. They let themselves be known be-
cause they are not altered by being known, because their principle of
indeterminacy no longer acts. This idea is important for all the ver-
sions of pastoral, for the pastoral figure is always ready to be the
critic; he not only includes everything but may in some unexpected
way know it.

Another range of his knowledge might be mentioned here. I am
not sure what arrangement of flower-beds is described in the last
verse, but it seems clear that the sun goes through the 'zodiac' of
flowers in one day, and that the bees too, in going from one bed to
another, reminding us of the labours of the first verse, pass all sum-
mer in a day. They compute their time as well as we in that though
their lives are shorter they too contract all experience into it, and

this makes the poet watch over large periods of time as well as space. So far he becomes Nature, he becomes permanent. It is a graceful finale to the all-in-one theme, but not, I think, very important; the crisis of the poem is in the middle.

Once you accept the Oxford edition's note you may as well apply it to the whole verse.

> Meanwhile the Mind, from pleasure less,
> Withdraws into its happiness;
> The Mind, that Ocean where each kind
> Does streight its own resemblance find;
> Yet it creates, transcending these,
> Far other worlds, and other Seas,
> Annihilating . . .

From pleasure less. Either 'from the lessening of pleasure'—'we are quiet in the country, but our dullness /125/ gives a sober and self-knowing happiness, more intellectual than that of the over-stimulated pleasures of the town' or 'made less by this pleasure'—'The pleasures of the country give a repose and intellectual release which make me less intellectual, make my mind less worrying and introspective.' This is the same puzzle as to the consciousness of the thought; the ambiguity gives two meanings to pleasure, corresponding to his Puritan ambivalence about it, and to the opposition between pleasure and happiness. *Happiness,* again, names a conscious state, and yet involves the idea of things falling right, happening so, not being ordered by an anxiety of the conscious reason. (So that as a rule it is a weak word; it is by seeming to look at it hard and bring out its implications that the verse here makes it act as a strong one.)

The same doubt gives all their grandeur to the next lines. The sea if calm reflects everything near it; the mind as knower is a conscious mirror. Somewhere in the sea are sea-lions and -horses and everything else, though they are different from land ones; the unconsciousness is unplumbed and pathless, and there is no instinct so strange among the beasts that it lacks its fantastic echo in the mind. In the first version thoughts are shadows, in the second (like the *green thought*) they are as solid as what they image; and yet they still correspond to something in the outer world, so that the poet's intuition is comparable to pure knowledge. This metaphor may reflect back so that *withdraws* means the tide going down; the *mind* is *less* now, but will return, and it is now that one can see the rock-pools. On the Freudian view of an Ocean, *withdraws* would make this repose in Nature a return to the womb; anyway it may mean either 'withdraws into self-contemplation' or /126/ 'withdraws altogether, into its mysterious processes of digestion.' *Streight* may mean 'packed together,' in the microcosm, or 'at once'; the beasts see their reflection (perhaps the root idea of the metaphor) as soon as they look for it; the calm of Nature gives the poet an immediate self-knowledge. But we have already had two entrancingly witty verses about the sublimation of sexual desire into a taste for Nature (I should not say that this theme was the main emotional drive behind the poem, but it takes up a large part of its overt thought), and the *kinds* look for their *resemblance*, in practice, out of a desire for *creation*; in the mind, at this fertile time for the poet, they can *find* it 'at once,' being 'packed together.' The transition from the beast and its reflection to the two pairing beasts implies a transition from the correspondences of thought with fact to those of thought with thought, to find which is to be creative; there is necessarily here a suggestion of rising from one 'level' of thought to another; and in the next couplet not only does the mind transcend the world it mirrors, but a sea, to which it is parallel, transcends both land and sea too, which implies self-consciousness and all the antinomies of philosophy. Whether or not you give *transcendent* the technical sense 'predicable of all categories' makes no great difference; in including everything in itself the mind includes as a detail itself and all its inclusions. And it is true that the sea reflects the *other worlds* of the stars; Donne's metaphor of the globe is in the background. Yet even here the double meaning is not lost; all land-beasts have their sea-beasts, but the sea also has the kraken; in the depths as well as the transcendence of the mind are things stranger than all the kinds of the world. /127/

Miss M. C. Bradbrook has pointed out to me that the next verse, while less triumphant, gives the process a more firmly religious interpretation.

> Here at the Fountains sliding foot,
> Or by some Fruit-trees mossy root,
> Casting the Bodies Vest aside,
> My Soul into the boughs does glide;
> There like a Bird it sits, and sings,
> Then whets, and combs its silver Wings;
> And, till prepar'd for longer flight,
> Waves in its Plumes the various Light.

The bird is the dove of the Holy Spirit and carries a suggestion of the rainbow of the covenant. By becoming inherent in everything he becomes a soul not pantheist but clearly above and apart from the world even while still living in it. Yet the paradoxes are still firmly maintained here, and the soul is as solid as the green thought. The next verse returns naturally and still with exultation to the jokes in favour of solitude against women.

Green takes on great weight here, as Miss Sackville West pointed out, because it has been a pet word of Marvell's before. To list the uses before the satires may seem an affection of pedantry, but shows how often the word was used; and they are pleasant things to look up. In the Oxford text: pages 12, l. 23; 17, l. 18; 25, l. 11; 27, l. 4; 38, l. 3; 45, l. 3; 46, l. 25; 48, l. 18; 49, l. 48; 70, l. 376; 71, l. 390; 74, l. 510; 122, l. 2. Less rich uses: 15, l. 18; 21, l. 44; 30, l. 55; 42, l. 14; 69, l. 339; 74, ll. 484, 496; 78, l. 628; 85, l. 82; 89, l. 94; 108, l. 196. It is connected here with grass, buds, children, an as yet virginal prospect of sexuality, and the peasant stock from which the great families emerge. The /128/ 'unfathomable' grass makes the soil fertile and shows it to be so; it is the humble, permanent, undeveloped nature which sustains everything, and to which everything must return. . . . /130/

To nineteenth-century taste the only really poetical verse of the poem is the central fifth of the nine; I have been discussing the sixth, whose dramatic position is an illustration of its very penetrating theory. The first four are a crescendo of wit, on the themes 'success or failure is not important, only the repose that follows the exercise of one's powers' and 'women, I am pleased to say, are no longer interesting to me, because nature is more /131/ beautiful.' One effect of the wit is to admit, and so make charming, the impertinence of the second of these, which indeed the first puts in its place; it is only for a time, and after effort among human beings, that he can enjoy solitude. The value of these moments made it fitting to pretend they were eternal; and yet the lightness of his expression of their sense of power is more intelligent, and so more convincing, than Wordsworth's solemnity on the same theme, because it does not forget the opposing forces.

> When we have run our Passions heat,
> Love hither makes his best retreat.
> The *Gods*, that mortal beauty chase,
> Still in a Tree did end their race.
> *Apollo* hunted *Daphne* so,
> Only that she might Laurel grow,

> And *Pan* did after *Syrinx* speed,
> Not as a Nymph, but for a Reed.

The energy and delight of the conceit has been sharpened or keyed up here till it seems to burst and transform itself; it dissolves in the next verse into the style of Keats. So his observation of the garden might mount to an ecstasy which disregarded it; he seems in this next verse to imitate the process he has described, to enjoy in a receptive state the exhilaration which an exercise of wit has achieved. But striking as the change of style is, it is unfair to empty the verse of thought and treat it as random description; what happens is that he steps back from overt classical conceits to a rich and intuitive use of Christian imagery. When people treat it as the one good 'bit' of the poem one does not know whether they have recognised that the Alpha and Omega of the verse are the Apple and the Fall. /132/

> What wond'rous Life in this I lead!
> Ripe Apples drop about my head;
> The Luscious Clusters of the Vine
> Upon my Mouth do crush their Wine;
> The Nectaren, and curious Peach,
> Into my hands themselves do reach;
> Stumbling on Melons, as I pass,
> Insnar'd with Flow'rs, I fall on Grass.

Melon, again, is the Greek for apple; 'all flesh is *grass*,' and its own *flowers* here are the snakes in it that stopped Eurydice. Mere grapes are at once the primitive and the innocent wine; the *nectar* of Eden, and yet the blood of sacrifice. *Curious* could mean 'rich and strange' (nature), 'improved by care' (art) or 'inquisitive' (feeling towards me, since nature is a mirror, as I do towards her). All these eatable beauties give themselves so as to lose themselves, like a lover, with a forceful generosity; like a lover they *ensnare* him. It is the triumph of the attempt to impose a sexual interest upon nature; there need be no more Puritanism in this use of sacrificial ideas than is already inherent in the praise of solitude; and it is because his repose in the orchard hints at such a variety of emotions that he is contemplating *all that's made*. Sensibility here repeats what wit said in the verse before; he tosses into the fantastic treasure-chest of the poem's thought all the pathos and dignity that Milton was to feel in his more celebrated Garden; and it is while this is going on, we are told in the next verse, that the mind performs its ambiguous and memorable *withdrawal*. For each of the three central verses he gives a twist to the screw of the microscope and is living in another world.

Questions

William Empson, a theoretician, mathematician and writer on literature and linguistics, does not confine his *Versions of Pastoral* simply to the literary genre. Buddhist theology and Sigmund Freud are used as foreground perspectives on "The Garden" along with the romantic sensibility of Wordsworth and Keats (p. 131) and Marvell's literary contemporaries Donne and Milton (p. 126).

Are these multiple perspectives reconciled, or are they simply associations made to illuminate single points? Is each treated with the same seriousness?

What is the effect of Empson's practice of seeing two readings to the phrase: "either . . . or" (p. 119, 124-25)?

Empson sees "The Garden," first and finally, as a poem that reconciles opposites: the conscious and unconscious states of mind. How does the critic's own image of the microscope at the end of this excerpt help to suggest a reconciliation of meanings, or levels of meaning?

Ruth Wallerstein

Marvell and the Various Light*

Before turning to *The Garden*, we ought to draw together what we
know as to explicit systematic Platonism in Marvell's poetry. The
cosmic conceptions of *On a Drop of Dew* and of the poems on Crom-
well's anniversary and death mark those poems as consciously Pla-
tonic, the first very explicitly, the second by the implications of its
invention. The elements of Platonism in a *Dialogue Between the
Resolved Soul and Created Pleasure* had been long since woven into
the texture of Christianity. But possibly a passage such as that I have
cited earlier from Ficino on the imagination, as well as the whole
infusion of the world of the senses into Renaissance art helps to ex-
plain the subtlety and sensuous precision of Marvell's version of the
theme. If I am right in my reading of *Upon Appleton House*, Marvell
has in that poem deliberately rejected self-deception as to sensuous
sublimation; he has rejected libertine surrender to passion; he
has not rejected frank delight in the /319/ beauty of the creatures.
But it is a delight in which immediate experience passes indefinably
into a concept of the meaning of that beauty. And to the organization
of his feeling a reading of the Victorines and St. Bonaventura or of
writers dependent upon them may have contributed. Whether *On a
Drop Of Dew* and *A Dialogue* preceded or followed *The Garden* we
do not know. *The Coronet* is closely connected with the first in form,
and all three are close in tone and imagery. Putting these impressions
together with the known date of the Cromwell poems, I suggest that
the poems on Cromwell's protectorate follow *The Garden*, but the
first of them at no great distance. This would agree with the obvious

*Reprinted from *Studies in Seventeenth Century Poetic*. Madison: The University
of Wisconsin Press, 1950, pp. 318-35, by permission of the publisher. © 1950 by
the Regents of the University of Wisconsin.

25

usual inference as to the date of that poem. To *The Garden* the
literature of the *hortus conclusus* among all this reading contributes
the most.

The Garden was written in a frame of mind in which profound
piety was the groundwork and in a spirit deeply habituated to a
Roman attitude of detachment, measure, responsiveness to the pat-
terns of social order. Marvell had for himself given up the world. But
this was not all. For at the same time he was in a state of greatly
intensified sensibility. Self-awareness flooded him. He was experienc-
ing and reflecting on the many ways in which the elements of
consciousness might find direction and equilibrium. *The Garden*,
like *Upon Appleton House*, reflects this complex feeling within the
most precise intellectual and artistic control of its material, its specific
theme as a poem.

The first two stanzas repeat in concentrated form the first move-
ment of *Upon Appleton House*, the theme of retirement.[1] The theme
is here stated first in terms of classical thought, praising withdrawal
from the fame which comes through public office to the statesman
and through public honor to the poet; and here tone and thought
remind us of Lipsius; then in Christian terms, describing the re-
covery of the self from the world's stain. And here the deep imagina-
tive influence of writ- /320/ ing such as that I have cited from
Richard of St. Victor, or Bonaventura forms the setting for his
experience, as is shown both by tone and I believe, by the pattern of
key words and concepts. This is the religious retirement, this is the
meditative joy in the creatures of mediaeval Christian Platonism. But
this theme of withdrawal, even in the statement, breaks into that
joyous and creative sense of expansion into nature toward which the
whole poem moves. For,

> All Flow'rs and all Trees do close
> To weave the Garlands of repose,

and

> Society is all but rude,
> To this delicious Solitude.

These stanzas, like all of the first four, express the transformation
or conversion of the mind. And as in *Upon Appleton House*, in the
garden warfare, but more subtly and speedily in single word meta-
phor rather than in prolonged simile, the poets use double images,

which are seen in one light by the world, in another by the resolved soul.

The next two stanzas express the aversion from passion. In them, particular recollections of St. Amant and the libertines are still teeming through Marvell's mind, I think.

The praise of the lady's red and white and the symbolization of all passion in it were very widespread in Renaissance literature. Spenser affords an example ready to hand; but *La Solitude* of Théophile de Viau contains the striking lines,

> Que ton teinct est de bonne grace!
> Qu'il est blanc, et qu'il est vermeil!

The description of the beloved of which these lines form part is set in imitation of St. Amant in the secret retreats of a forest, the primitive haunt of innocence:

> Jamais la justice en courroux
> Icy de criminels ne cherche. /321/
> Icy l'amour faict ses estudes;
> Venus y dresse des autels.

It is the haunt of the amorous gods; it is the haunt in which he may enjoy Corine far from all eyes but those of Cupid. Is not Marvell's

> No red nor white was ever seen
> So am'rous as this lovely green

an answer to this or similar passages? M. Legouis cites Spenser's *Hymne in Honour of Beautie*, stanza XI; but Spenser only denies that it is the outward beauty which seizes us, without condemning red and white; Spenser carries us back through red and white to the form from which the red and white spring. Marvell turns us sharply from all earthly love to heavenly.

The core for the meaning of *green* in this passage is to be found in Mr. D. C. Allen's article on "Symbolic Color in the Literature of the Renaissance."[2] Green had been in the Middle Ages in secular thought a symbol of youth or joy—one remembers Nausicaä as a young growing thing—but also of fickleness. But in Platonism it had become the symbol of hope. And in mediaeval Platonism we can see the transformation taking place, Easter absorbing the hymns of spring, and the renewal of nature becoming the symbol of hope in the Resurrection.

Mr. Allen cites Alciati, "Spei color est viridis," and the Italian writer on color symbolism, Giovanni Rinaldi, "Allegrezza e speranza se la speranza istessa se adorna di verde vesta, e questo per mostrarci che essa sola e cagione d'ogni nostra felicita e allegrezza." And Allen goes on to say green is regularly used by the Pléiade as a symbol of hope. Even in Dante, who knew Bonaventura, I find it approaching symbolic use: *mentre che la speranza ha fior del verde.* M. Legouis cites St. John of the Cross that hope is a "prado de verduraz." The contrast Marvell here makes had already been made by Marini in his *Della Speranza*, to my earlier citation from which the reader may /322/ turn; though Marini's poem is a mere series of conceits upon a concept and Marvell's a personal lyric, *Della Speranza* offers a striking parallel to Marvell's theme and to his symbolism. There is also a tantalizing echo of a popular Italian saying which might have clung to Marvell's memory, and to which we are led by the later lines,

> Annihilating all that's made
> To a green Thought in a green Shade.

In Italy, candles set on altars were often colored green at the lower ends; and in the literature of color symbolism Fulvio Pellegrino (Morato) in his *Significato dei Colori e de Mazzoli*, goes with considerable antiquarian lore into the origin of this practice to prove that green is not the color of hope but of failure of hope. He certainly seems to show that the custom was the origin of some uses of the term green, as in Sonnet XXXIII of Petrarch. His own color theories he embodied in a sonnet in answer to one by Serafino. And this sonnet begins with the line, *Il color verde ridutto a niente dimostra.*[3] His sonnet, as he himself tells us, won him only ill will; and Serafino's interpretations, in which green is hope or love, remained the accepted ones. But could the line have been seen by Marvell and remembered, even while he forgot Pellegrino's interpretation, or is it the record of a popular saying that he might have heard in Italy? Carducci and Ferrari cite a reference by Leopardi to the candle and to the popular saying to explain the line in Petrarch: "Dicesi tolto della candela tinta in verde nel fine, ove giunto il lume poco sta ad esser del tolto consumato: E piu de parlar familiare." The candle itself had been cited by Daniello in his commentary on Petrarch.

The use of green in this sense of hope marks the philosophic focus of Marvell's thought in this poem. In *Upon Appleton House* in "this yet green, yet growing ark," the adjective has /323/ wider, more general connotations of living, springing life and expresses a more undetermined thought. These connotations are still present as overt ones in *The Garden*, especially in the later stanza, and keep directly before our senses the experience on which Marvell rests his thought. For that reason closer still than the passages I have referred to is Stradling's translation of Lipsius, for there symbol is only suggested, if at all, as a hovering implication of immediate experience. And closest of all in blending of experience and symbol is a passage in Hugh of St. Victor's book of the creatures from the description of the beauty of the world:

> Postremo super omne pulchrum viride, quomodo animos intuentium rapit; quando vere novo, nova quadam vita germina prodeunt, et erecta sursum in spiculis suis quasi deorsum morte calcata ad imaginem futurae resurrectionis in lucem pariter erumpunt? Sed quid de operibus Dei loquimur? etiam humanae industriae fucos adulterina quadam sapientia fallentes ocubos tantopere miramur?[4]

In this setting, the full and precise religious implication of Marvell's term *am'rous* and its relation to the tradition of the *raptus* of profane love by sacred, which goes back to Origen, needs no comment.

Marvell's Latin version is closer in expression to neo-Latin poetry than to the French poetry he may well have had running through his memory, and the roll of the names in the Latin of the mistresses banned from the garden specifically evokes Horace, Ovid, and the elegists: Neaera, Chloe, Faustina, Corinna. But these poets had already been evoked by Théophile, for his mistress is Corine. And *On a Drop of Dew* has shown us how Marvell would think in terms of a contemporary or of an ancient tradition or idiom according as he wrote in English or Latin.[5] The carving of the names on the trees as a symbol of bringing passion into nature was running in Marvell's mind; for it is half transformed already in *Upon the Hill and Grove at /324/ Bill-borow*. The concept was doubtless widespread. It had been used by St. Amant, in a perhaps more sophisticated way than by Orlando.

In the Latin version of Marvell's poem, it is the burning Ovidian passions of the gods which are evoked with some fulness of allusion. And the release from their fury is perhaps reminiscent of Latin visions of halcyon days. The opening line of the English stanza, "when we have run our passion's heat," in the literal sense of *passion's heat* possibly alludes, as Mr. King has suggested, to the torch of Cupid.[6] But perhaps both in the literal meaning and in the figurative picture of the race *heat* has rather the more simple and broadly symbolic meaning of the weary and consuming contest of the world and the appetites.

The religious note is, as yet, however, firmly but only lightly present in the stanza. It is the joy of art which the quiet of nature brings if she bring anything but her own joy. If Marvell had already turned his thought to Herbert and to his own *Coronet*, religion and art were not separate in his thought. But yet it is purely the classical sense of detachment, freedom, and joy in art which the lines express. And Pan will play this reed only to himself. Perhaps as Marvell wrote he remembered again St. Amant's

> O que j'ayme la solitude!
> C'est l'element des bons esprits,
> C'est par elle que j'ay compris
> L'art d'Apollon sans nulle estude,

for Marvell shares with St. Amant as much as he rejects. Perhaps only, the more general commonplace that it is in solitude that poets are inspired, a commonplace cited as such, for instance, by Erasmus in his early *De Contemptu Mundi*, in defense of monasticism and repopularized by the rhetorician Pontanus. One recalls how Pan was allegorized in the Renais- /325/ sance, but that seems irrelevant here. One may also just fleetingly recall that Pan and his companions had had their place in the happy garden of Bernardus Sylvestris, recall it not in specific relation to Marvell but to remind one's self how wide and how radical within Christian limits the justification of nature might be. That Marvell's own poetic impulse owed a great quickening to Nun Appleton seems sure.

Then with startling suddenness we are absorbed in nature herself.

> What wond'rous Life is this I lead!

In the first stanza of the group formed by v, vi, and vii we are still in the life of the senses. There is an almost sensual delight in the bounty of nature to taste and touch. One thinks at once of the fruit passage in *The Bermudas:*

> He makes the Figs our mouths to meet;
> And throws the Melons at our feet
> But Apples plants of such a price,
> No Tree could ever bear them twice.

But this vision of God's bounty is utterly stripped of the sensuous intensity of the ripe apples dropping on the head, the luscious clusters of the vine crushing their wine on his lips, the very feel of the nectaren and curious peach in the hand with which the *Garden* stanza glows.

Many impulses meet in the stanza. It must be read first, I think, in the light of the ivy stanza in *Upon Appleton House*. It affirms the delight of the senses in nature; it rejects the conversion of this delight to erotic enhancement. It returns back from passion to the pure joy in the creatures. There are two French poems, of St. Amant and of Théophile, so suggestive for these lines that we ought to have them in mind as a type of thing which Marvell might well have read and which might have contributed to his own handling of his experience. /326/

The following lines from St. Amant's *Le Melon* indicate the sensuous delight and the tone as a whole of that poem.

LE MELON

> Quelle odeur sens-je en cette chambre?
> Quel doux parfum de musc et d'ambre
> Me vient le cerveau resjouir
> Et tout le coeur espanouir?
> Ha! bon Dieu! j'en tombe en extase:
>
>   . . .
>
> Qu'est-ce donc? Je l'ay descouvert
> Dans ce panier rempli de vert:
> C'est un MELON, où la nature,
> Par une admirable structure,
> A voulu graver à l'entour
> Mille plaisans chiffres d'amour,
> Pour claire marque à tout le monde
> Que d'une amitié sans seconde
> Elle cherit ce doux manger,
>
>   . . .
>
> Baillez-le-moy, je vous en prie,
> Que j'en commette idolatrie:
> O! quelle odeur! qu'il est pesant!
> Et qu'il me charme en le baisant!

After a brief humorous prayer that the melon may not be found to contain any of "le deaut des gens d'aujourd' huy," there is a full blazon as of a damosel or a Corine of the beauty of the interior of the fruit and a rhapsody upon its power to surpass all the precisely listed delights of the other fruits. Finally, a derivation of its growth on Parnassus introduces an extensive and not happy myth in another key and in another verse form.

Théophile's praise of the fruits is set in a more serious poem, the *Lettre à son frère*, and it is marked by tender recollection rather than by lively humorous sensibility. Lamenting his hard condition and his despair amid the ill wishes of his enemies, he /327/ reflects that his life is in the hands of Heaven and not in theirs. "J'espere toutefois au Ciel." Perhaps his destiny is about to change,[7] and despite all that his adversaries can do, out of the midst of the depression in which his senses can take delight only in what makes them sad, he has not yet lost the hope that before he dies he shall see Boussères and the countryside of his childhood.

> Je cueilleray ces abricots,
> Les fraises à couleur de flames,
> Dont nos bergers font des escots
> Qui seroient icy bons aux dames,
> Et ces figues et ces melons
> Dont la bouche des aquilons
> N'a jamais sceu baiser l'escorce.
> Et ces jaunes muscats si chers,
> Que jamais la gresle ne force
> Dans l'asyle de nos rochers.
>
> Je verray sur nos grenadiers
> Leurs rouges pommes entr'ouvertes,
> Où le Ciel, comme à ses lauriers,
> Garde tousjours des fueilles vertes.
> Je verray ce touffu jasmin
> Qui fait ombre à tout le chemin
> D'une assez spacieuse allee,
> Et la parfume d'une fleur
> Qui conserve dans la gelee
> Son odorat et sa couleur.
>
> Je reverray fleurir nos prez;
> Je leur verray couper les herbes;
> Je verray quelque temps apres
> Le paysan couché sur les gerbes;

But in Marvell, we have not only turned from the fever of the city to the tranquil friendliness of the country with a sly reminder, to a reader much versed in Renaissance discussion of fame, with what labor fame is to be earned. His fruits are not /328/ earned by the sweat of our brow. We have in them a joy greater than the joy of St. Amant. A gathering image of Paradise keeps suggesting to our fancy a thought which rises to the surface in the last line:

> Stumbling on Melons, as I pass,
> Insnar'd with Flow'rs, I fall on Grass.

Though the apple was the instrument of our Fall, Marvell is not
thinking of that, but only of the riches of the fruits and flowers of
Eden and of the earth. The cause is really woman. By her are en-
snared the libertines who ought to love only the garden. St. Amant's
verses suggest to us the humorous or burlesque tone, now turned by
Marvell to a mockery of the French poet himself, in which we ought
to read the lines. Yet with all this background in mind, to our modern
ear there is something of violence in the stanza. This delight of the
senses has for the moment taken possession of Marvell. And the sensu-
ous pleasure of the garden is only a "pleasure less." Neo-Platonic
concepts of the relation of this specific beauty to the ideal beauty are
used just so far as a neo-Platonic view can be precisely filled with
Marvell's own experience and can add to that experience, as it were,
a fourth dimension of significance.

He has entered into the mind's own world, and the figures cease to
be the figures of double value which in the earlier stanzas mark and
keep constantly at work in the poem the choice between two worlds.
The *hortus conclusus*, the enclosed garden, is the soul herself. The
quaint conception "That all Animals of the Land, are in their kind in
the Sea" is an emblem for the mind's possession of the forms of all
things, forms through which it turns to their essence.

> Yet it creates, transcending these
> Far other Worlds and other Seas

may be read in the light of the passage from Ficino on the imagina-
tion quoted earlier, telling how things take on a larger /329/ beauty
as they pass from individual objects to species in the phantasy,
whence the mind receives them. *Annihilating* I take with Mr. Margo-
liouth in the sense of "reducing the whole material world to an
immaterial thought," with something of a second meaning, consider-
ing all the world of created things as nothing compared to the hope
of the eternal world brought to me by the beauty and the symbolism
of this green shade.[8] He is still close to the immediate perception of
the "yet green, yet growing ark" of *Upon Appleton House*. Yet his
primary intention is here symbolic, marking the difference between
the two poems. And the green thought is clearly that hope to which
Fate's whole lottery is one blank and whose chase is

The God of nature in the field of Grace.

The meditation on values and the definition completed, Marvell gives us in the next stanza an actual experience of transcendence, of which the meditation itself is a part. For is not the *various light* the multifold reflection in nature of the one essential Light from which nature springs? The closest analogue is that I have already quoted from Bonaventura.

> And as a certain light mixed with opacity is the way, so it is the way leading to the exemplar. Just as you have seen that a ray entering through the window is colored in various ways by the various colors of the various parts of the glass, so the divine ray shines variously in the particular creatures, and with various properties.[9]

Others may be found in Plotinus:

> That great soul must stand pictured before another soul, one not mean, a soul that has become worthy to look, emancipate from the lure, from all that binds its fellows into bewitchment, holding itself in quietude. Let not merely the enveloping body be at peace, body's turmoil stilled, but all that lies around, earth at peace, and sea at peace, air and the very heavens. Into that heaven, all that rest, let the great soul be conceived to roll inward at every point, penetrating, permeating, from all sides pouring its light. As the rays of the sun throwing their brilliance upon a lowering cloud make it gleam all /330/ gold, so the soul entering the material expanse of the heavens has given life, has given immortality: what was abject it has lifted up; and the heavenly system, moved now in endless motion by the soul that leads it in wisdom, has become a living and a blessed thing; the soul domiciled within, it takes worth where, before the soul, it was stark body—clay and water—or, rather, the blankness of Matter, the absence of Being, and, as an author says, "the execration of the Gods." . . .

> Conferring—but how? As itself possessing them or not? How can it convey what it does not possess, and yet if it does possess how is it simplex? And if, again, it does not, how is it the source of the manifold?
> A single, unmanifold emanation we may very well allow—how even that can come from a pure unity may be a problem, but we may always explain it on the analogy of the irradiation from a luminary—but a multitudinous production raises question. . . .

> It must be a circumradiation—produced from the Supreme but from the Supreme unaltering—and may be compared to the brilliant light encircling the sun and ceaselessly generated from that unchanging substance.[10]

And others in the *Dialoghi d' Amore* of Leone Ebreo:

> On the contrary, being unable to understand the pure unity of the divine object, it multiplies it relatively and by reflection into three, for a clear and single object cannot be impressed upon another less clear (and more complex) than itself unless its own exceeding brightness be multiplied into several lesser lights. Behold the sun, when it casts its rays upon the clouds, forming the bow: into how many colours its light is transformed by them reflecting it, or by water or a mirror. And in itself it is pure light without any colour of its own, yet it transcends and contains every other hue; so divine formality, which is perfect unity and simplicity in itself, cannot be imaged in another except by the reflection of its light and the multiplication of its formality.

Or again: /331/

> SOFIA: this sublime abstraction seems to mean that from the one depend the many separate causes. But give me an example. . . .
> FILONE: I recall that I have given you a visible example of the sun and all the particular corporeal lights and colors. For though all depend on him, and in him exist as ideas all the essences of all the colors and lights of the universe, in all their degrees, yet in him they are not multiplied and divided. . . . And you see how when the pure sun imprints itself on a moist cloud opposite it, it makes the bow called iris. . . .[11]

Thus the soul of Marvell waves in its thought the various light of the creatures until she shall fly to God.

Just possibly there is in this stanza again some echo of St. Amant's *La Solitude* and of what the impulse of reading him may have contributed to this very different attitude of Marvell's.

> Que je trouve doux le ravage
> De ces fiers torrens vagabonds,
> Qui se precipitent par bonds
> Dans ce vallon vert et sauvage!
> Puis glissant sous les arbrisseaux,
>
> .   .   .
>
> Que j'aime ce marets paisible!
>
> .   .   .
>
> Là, cent mille oyseaux aquatiques
> Vivent, sans craindre, en leur repos,
> Le giboyeur fin et dispos,

Avec ses mortelles practiques.
L'un, tout joyeux d'un si beaux jour,
S'amuse à becqueter sa plume;
L'autre allentit le feu d'amour
Qui dans l'eau mesme se consume,
Et prennent tous innocemment
Leur plaisir en cet élément.[12]

But for Marvell the creatures have become emblems. And yet not that, for an emblem is a detached object of meditation. Here at the very moment of meeting of Marvell's exquisite sensuous perception and his habitual feeling and his thought, the /332/ bird has ceased to be an emblem and his experience of it has become an immediate psychological experience, a symbol in the modern psychological sense of an organism of thought concretized around a particular intuition, and in the sense at least half implied by Richard of St. Victor. His aesthetic joy in some actual bird passes into a symbol of his soul's joy in the creation.

Thus, in a modified neo-Platonic psychology, the mind has a vision so far as is possible while she is in this life of the divine beauty wherein she had her origin. And yet I would not suggest that Marvell wished to describe any special religious experience. The experience he would awaken in us he describes precisely, a tranquilizing, an enlargement, a unification of consciousness, in which what might have been only an evanescent experience was fixed and given content by the religious thought which entered to fill it. He interpreted it as a moment of pure intelligential activity; in that sense an ecstasy. Yet I am convinced we should be mistaken to think of it as a withdrawal from the body in quite so explicit and, if I may say so, local a sense as Donne describes in his poem. Rather it lies halfway between that meaning and Milton's when he speaks of the ecstasy of music. It is in perfect keeping with Marvell's strict sense of the limitation of knowledge, an understanding of the one light still only through the various lights, but an absolutely dependable intuition; one in which the infusion of grace has its part.

Whether in mediaeval hexaëmeral literature or in Florentine Platonism, Platonic psychology is synthesized with Christian revelation. And what is in neo-Platonic psychology the separation of the soul from the Divine Intelligence is in Christian history The Fall of Man and Original Sin. Are we for a moment carried, in our recovered Innocence, back behind the Flaming Sword? And is there in the opening lines of stanza VII a shadowy background picture of Eden which catches up the suggestion of stanza V? /333/

> Here at the Fountains sliding foot,
> Or at some Fruit-trees mossy root . . . .

The student of English literature can hardly help looking forward to the opening of Milton's picture of Paradise and to the literature which lies back of it.

> Out of the fertil ground he caus'd to grow
> All trees of noblest kind for sight, smell, taste;
> Southward through *Eden* went a River large.

The tone of the Biblical reminiscences in *Upon Appleton House* affords a fruitful parallel. Yet if we see this picture, it is only in the barest fleeting suggestion. For *The Garden* is not an allegory of the Fall of Man. It is a lyric study of Marvell's experience. And the three stanzas have moved from imagination and a state of normal "discursive" thought in stanza v, in which the mind collects and compares many views of the world, into a state of ecstacy. It is only as the mind falls back from ecstacy that the thought of Eden becomes articulate.

And it is then an Eden from which man has long been banished, and the recollection of which only defines for him his present forlorn state.

As the moment of contemplation fades, the neo-Platonic pattern which came within the circle of the poem to interpret the contemplation moves out of view too. The condemnation of passion which has played so large a part in the poem is seen in stanza VIII in one traditional mediaeval light. It is asserted with a crisp personal asperity.

> Wommannes conceil broughte us first to wo
> And made Adam fro Paradys to go.

The lines are so swift, spring so inevitably from the tide of feeling of the poem that to bring in any association from without seems heavy-handed. Yet did Marvell fleetingly and whimsically recall a rabbinic legend cited in Leone Ebreo and in /334/ Browne, and therefore we know current, that in Paradise before the Fall Adam was an androgyne?

From this moment of wayward brooding on man's condition we return swiftly in the last stanza to the tranquilty of our Yorkshire garden. We are back in the world, a world that has become by our choice of retirement, ordered and innocent. Marvell perhaps remembers, as Miss Bradbrook and Miss Lloyd Thomas have pointed out, the books of garden emblems. But at least since Gregory of Nyssa that

citizenly bee has inhabited the enclosed garden. The poet has re-
turned also, in returning to the world, to the double image and pun.

> And, as it works, th' industrious Bee
> Computes its time as well as we.

Order is one through all the world of the creatures.

Does he remember, too, Virgil's bees? For the Latin sense of social
order is not far from Marvell's thought. And does this humanist also
just possibly remember his Elyot's *Booke of the Gouernour*, in which
the personal and the social self are so deeply integrated? One could
hardly find a more characteristic representation than in Elyot of the
twofold concept of the individual in English Renaissance thought.
And it is at the heart of Marvell's tradition, and of all his thought
about the state. Even Venice as an example of a happily balanced
state is present to Elyot's mind, as so probably to Marvell's.

> For who can denie but that all thynge in heuen and erthe is gouerned
> by one god, by one perpetuall ordre, by one prouidence? . . . and to
> descende downe to the erthe, in a litell beest, whiche of all other is
> moste to be maruayled at, I meane the Bee, is lefte to man by nature,
> as it semeth, a perpetuall figure of a iuste gouernance or rule; who
> hath amonge them one principall Bee for theyr gouernour, . . . and
> with that all the residue prepare them to labour, and fleeth abrode,
> gatheryng nothing but what shall be swete and profitable, all though
> they sitte often tymes on herbes and other thinges that be venomous
> and stynkinge . . . . /335/

> But what nede we to serche so ferre from us, [for instances of disorder
> in states that try to live as it were in a communaltie] sens we haue
> sufficient examples nere unto us? . . . After that the Saxons by treason
> had expelled out of Englande the Britons, which were the auncient
> inhabitantes, this realme was deuyded in to sondry regions or kyng-
> domes. O what mysery was the people than in. O howe this most noble
> Isle of the worlde was decerpt and rent in pieces. . . .

Notes

1 It is hard not to write as though *The Garden* certainly followed *Appleton
   House*. It is of course possible that it marked a moment of concentration
   within the formation of *Appleton House*. But the detail of the "sliding
   foot" repeated in the two poems is likely to have gone from the literal
   experience to the figurative use, as Miss Bradbrook and Miss Lloyd
   Thomas have observed, and the interest in neo-Platonic psychology looks
   toward the second Cromwell poem of 1655.

2 "Symbolic Color in the Literature of the Renaissance," *Philological Quarterly*, XV (1936), 81-92.

3 N.p., 1599.

4 Last, above all, beautiful green. How it seizes the mind of the gazers, when in a new spring the seeds advance in a new life, and erectly upward as if in symbols, death being trampled downward, they burst into light in the image of the future resurrection. But why shall we speak of the works of God, when we wonder so much at even the colors of human contriving which deceive our eyes with an adulterated wisdom, as it were?—*Didascalia* (*ed. cit.*), Bk. VII, Chap. XIII.

5 See pp. 163-64.

6 King, "Some Notes on Andrew Marvell's *Garden*," *English Studies*, XX, 118-21.

7 Reference to heaven in Théophile, as Antoine Adam has shown (*Théophile de Viau*), does not carry theistic implications but a belief in Fate and in a self-developing nature.

8 More broadly, *annihilate* is a term used by St. John of the Cross to express the dark night of the senses. Sir Thomas Browne, in a somewhat cursory view, equates the term with others, including ecstasy, used by mystical writers for mystical transcendence of the body.

9 *Hexaëmeron* (*ed cit.*), Sermon XII, p. 88: *Sicut tu vides quod radius intrans fenestram diversimode coloratur, secundum colores diversos, diversarum partium vitri; radius divinus in singulis creaturis diversimode et diversis proprietatibus refulget.*

10 *Enneads*, IV, Tractate III, secs. 9, 10, 17, tr. by Stephen McKenna (London, 1917-1930).

11 *Ed. cit.*

12 Stanzas IV, V, VI.

Questions

Ruth Wallerstein calls this section of her book "Marvell and the Various Light." She explains: "the *various light* is the multifold reflection in nature of the one essential Light from which nature springs" (p. 329). As this selection proceeds, following "The Garden" more or less stanza by stanza, Marvell's poem is read as a multifold reflection of other literary, philosophical, and theological writing. Miss Wallerstein's critical approach differs from Empson's, however, in that she is more rigidly historical. The contexts of French libertinism and renaissance Neo-Platonism are established as prior to or contemporary with Marvell, and the texts associated with "The Garden" are treated as potential, or probable, source materials.

What further comparisons should be drawn between the critical methods of Empson and Ruth Wallerstein? Is either classifiable as a "New Critic"?

Miss Wallerstein herself has a very difficult style. Are her various historical associations sufficiently reconciled, so as to suggest a view of the poem as a whole?

In our opinion, part of Miss Wallerstein's purpose is to expose her readers to certain poems and prose works which she considers important both in themselves and as they contribute to an understanding of seventeenth-century English literature.* To what extent do you consider her readings of St. Amant, for example, appreciative, rather than strictly studious and illustrative?

---

*If this is true, her intentions come close to the discipline of "Comparative Literature."

Milton Klonsky

A Guide Through the Garden*

Andrew Marvell's "The Garden" may be considered, figuratively, (for the poem itself *is* a figure) as an arboretum where the seeds of neo-Platonic Ideas are brought to a metaphysical bloom. It is a pastoral poem, yet a pastoral whose Nature is Ideas and whose image is words. In structure, the figure of "The Garden" is a conceit elaborated from a single essential metaphor, seed-like, so that its revelation to us is an unravelling of itself, the flowering of one rooted Idea: *A Garden in time is the neo-Platonic Realm of First Forms.*

Through a conflation of the Realm of First Forms with the Garden of Eden, its Biblical counterpart, this Idea-Metaphor is drawn even further by Marvell. The complete *figure* (and here is the paradox) is taken *literally*, the identification of both terms is complete.

But there is still a deeper involution of insight, as though a mirrored eye should see itself seeing itself, for this image of Marvell's is the reflection of a similar image from Plotinus' *Enneads*, the image of an image, a metaphor refracted by an allegory—an allegory in which Plotinus envisions how the Reason-Principle (Zeus) impregnates Nature (Aphrodite) with the *Logoi Spermatikoi* of Forms.

A Garden is a place of beauty and a glory of wealth; all the loveliness that Zeus maintains takes its splendour from the Reason-Principle within him; for all this beauty is the radiation of the Divine Intellect upon the Divine Soul, which it has penetrated. What could the Garden of Zeus indicate but the images of his Being and splendours of his Glory? And what could these divine beauties and splen- /17/ dours be but the Ideas streaming from him? (*Enneads,* III, 5, 9)

*Reprinted from *Sewanee Review*, LVII (Winter, 1950), 16-28, by permission of the publisher and the author. Copyright by The University of the South.

Although the metaphor derived from this passage is never explicitly stated by Marvell, its implications are drawn into a conceit so hermetic and exclusive that "The Garden" would be impossible to penetrate without its guidance.

II

> How vainly men themselves amaze
> To win the Palm, the Oke, or Bayes;
> And their uncessant Labours see
> Crown'd from some single Herb or Tree.
> *Whose short and narrow verged Shade*
> *Does prudently their Toyles upbraid;*
> While all Flow'rs and all Trees do close
> To weave the Garlands of Repose.

The image of Ideas is words and symbols. At the very start of the poem, an apparently straightforward statement on the vanity of ambitious toil is wrenched by the use of puns, like fracturing mirrors, into a multiplicity of meanings—but with all of these meanings controlled by the basic metaphor which, in turn, is formed by them.

"Shade" (which reappears crucially later on) is defined as a place not exposed to sunlight *and* a vital essence or soul; "Toyles" as harsh labors *and* the twisting of branches; and "upbraid" as to chide *and* to weave upwards. If the double meanings of all these words are maintained, then the third couplet is amphibolous and a sentence without a fixed subject: "Whose" may refer either to the vain men or to the "single Herb or Tree." Or, as it does, to both considered as one.

Analyzed separately, there are two sets of readings for each referent of "Whose": 1) The cramped, "short and narrow verged" Soul of the tree of ambition chides the vain men for /18/ their toil. And, the Soul of the vain men, having entered into the tree and been crowned by it, now complains of its tree-soul's twisted being. 2) The tree of ambition, whose shadow has been shortened and narrowed by the "upbraided" toils of its branches, is self-mutilated and self-condemned. And, the narrowed Soul of the vain men, with an after-wisdom, regrets the ambitious toil which degraded it.

But in order to join both interpretations, the Soul of the tree and the Soul of the vain men must be considered as the same. The figure must be taken *literally*, and the literal meaning *figuratively*. For only by metaphor can the Idea of the vain men be transubstantiated into the root and sap of the Garden.

The souls which enter "the Palme, the Oke, or Bayes" are self-condemned because they willfully rejected the contemplation of the Reason-Principle for a life of sensation and action. Plotinus believes this audacity to be the original sin—the Tolma which, in the Bible, degraded man and nature.

> By advancing on a path different from, and opposed to the contemplation of Intelligence, the universal soul begets an image of herself, sensation and the nature of growth. . . . Nevertheless, nothing is detached or separated from the superior principle which begets her. Thus the human soul seems to reach down to within that of plant growth. She descends therein inasmuch as the plant derives growth from her. (V, ii, 1)

Those who seek the rewards of action are further defined by Plotinus as "men too weak for speculation who, in action, seek a shadow of speculation and reason. . . . What man indeed who could contemplate truth would go and contemplate its image?" (III, viii, 4) Marvell leaves them squirming in their own spiritual cramp. But the fall from grace brought about by the soul's entanglement in the briars of sense and action is a /19/ theme which he takes up again, rehearsing and reweaving its implications into the great climax of the poem.

It must be made plain, however, that even though the vegetal order is the lowest manifestation of Soul in the world, in the Plotinus-Marvell metaphor *all* Ideas and Souls, good and evil, are rooted in the Garden. They are not degraded by growing there. The men of action who inhabit "the Oke, the Palme, or Bayes" would, outside the enchanted plot of the metaphor, descend into "gluttonous and lascivious animals where all is appetite and satiation of appetite. While those who in their pleasures have not even lived by sensation, but have gone their way in a torpid grossness, become mere growing things, for this lethargy is the entire act of the vegetative, and such men have been busy betreeing themselves." (III, iv, 2) But here we are concerned only with Marvell's hypostatized Garden of all Souls and Ideas, and not with the outer Jungle explored by Plotinus.

"Repose," the word which completes the first stanza, turns by a natural path away from those Toyling and upbraiding Shades, and into a grove of Quiet and Innnocense, the Garden state before the fall.

> Fair Quiet, have I found thee here,
> And Innocense thy Sister dear!
> Mistaken long, I sought you then
> In busy Companies of Men.

> Your sacred Plants, if here below,
> Only among the Plants will grow.
> Society is all but rude,
> To this delicious solitude.

If the Forms of Quiet and Innocense are "here below" then they must enter the plants and be planted, their essence taking root in the formal ground of the Garden, for only here, among Ideas, can their nature be realized. "Innocense" and "Quiet," /20/ whose Names are unviolated and undisturbed, must, therefore, exist in solitude (as one) in a consubstantial unity of thought and object. Such a Garden solitude where thought and the object of thought copulate in Platonic love is, truly, as Marvell says it is, "delicious"—with all the erotic Latin of that word exposed.

> No white nor red was ever seen
> So am'rous as this lovely green.
> Fond lovers, cruel as their Flame,
> Cut in these trees their Mistress name.
> Little, Alas, they know, or heed,
> How far these Beauties hers exceed. . . .

Just as the "Flame" of these cruel lovers is both love and the person loved, who are identified, so the Ideational trees of the Garden are united with their names, they are their Names.

> Fair trees! where s'eer your barks I wound,
> No name shall but your own be found.

The promise is kept—for these last two lines (and the whole poem as well) are carved in the tree-Ideas which inspire and substantiate them. The Platonic identification of Name and Object in a formal hierarchy is all that matters here, though matter itself, as Yeats once said, is but a spume that plays upon this paradigm. Plotinus is explicit:

When we cut the twigs or branches of a tree, where goes the plant soul that was in them? She returns to her principle, for no local difference separates her therefrom. If we cut or burn the root, whither goes the power of growth present therein? It returns to the plant power of the Universal soul, which does not change place and does not cease being where it was. (V, ii, 2)

In the next stanza, the mode of abstract passion is further /21/ advanced; and here the very objects of love are transmuted, their essence becoming the plants of the Garden. The mortal creatures Daphne and Syrinx who aroused the lust of the Gods were possessed by them—but only as Ideas in their Platonic love. Eros and Agape are sisters under the skin.

> Apollo hunted Daphne so
> Only that she might laurel grow.
> And Pan did after Syrinx speed
> Not as a nymph but for a reed.[1]

To characterize the chase after fugitive lust, Marvell employs the pejorative figure of a running meet, violent action for a finite reward —an image which recalls the vain men in the first stanza who win "the Palme, the Oke or Bayes." But even ambition on the part of the Gods is condemned.

> When we have run our Passions heat
> Love hither makes his best retreat.
> The Gods, that mortal beauty chase,
> Still in a tree did end their race.

Puns on the words "heat," "retreat," "chase," "race," support the double image. The Gods who chase "mortal beauty" are not only Pan and Apollo but, also, Christ crucified, who came in the last of the "race" of Gods. After the frenzy of love for humanity, all at last complete and cross their passion in a tree, rooted in Quiet and Solitude, and are "still."

The suggestion of Biblical imagery here is fulfilled in the next stanza by a further extension of the basic metaphor in which the neo-Platonic Realm of First Forms becomes the Garden of Eden. With the ripe round feminine forms of apples, peaches, nectarines, grapes, and melons, (imagery of the Song of Solomon), the sensuality which had been steadily rising up to now is climactically discharged. /22/

> What wondrous Life is this I lead!
> Ripe apples drop about my head;
> The luscious clusters of the Vine
> Upon my mouth do crush their Wine;
> The Nectaren, and curious Peach,

---

[1] cf. Thomas Carew's "A Rapture," 130-39.

> Into my hands themselves do reach;
> Stumbling on Melons, as I pass,
> Insnar'd with Flowers, I fall on Grass.

Until the last couplet, Marvell's protagonist is innocent of any corruptive action—the apples drop about his head, the grapes of wine crush themselves upon his mouth, the peach and the nectarine grope into his hands—all things come to succor him. But when he acts to assert his own desires, then he is ensnared with flowers, stumbles on melons (Gr. apples—the forbidden fruit?) and falls on grass. Grass and flowers to represent the transitory beauty of the senses are very old tropes; for example, they figure prominently in the Bible.

> And the voice said Cry. And he said, What shall I cry? All flesh is grass, and all the goodliness thereof is as the flower of the field: The grass withereth, the flower fadeth, but the word of our God shall stand forever. (Isaiah, XL, 6)

"How does it happen," asks Plotinus, "that souls forget their paternal divinity?" His answer is curiously like that of the Bible.

> The origin of their evil is audacity, generation, the primary diversity, and the desire to belong to none but themselves. As soon as they have enjoyed the pleasures of an independent life, and by largely making use of their powers of self-direction, they advanced on the road that led them astray from their principle, and now they have arrived at such an apostasy from the divinity that they are even ignorant that they derive their life from him. . . . This /23/ ignorance is, therefore, caused by excessive valuation of external objects, and their scorn of themselves. The mere admiration and quest after what is foreign implies, on the soul's part, an acknowledgement of self-depreciation. (V, i, 1)

After death the soul and the body and the mind are dissevered.

> Meanwhile, the Mind, from pleasure less
> Withdraws into its happiness;
> The Mind, that Ocean where each kind
> Does streight its own resemblance find. . . .

Once delivered and free from sensation, ("from pleasure less,") the mind retires according to Plotinus "within the superior Power." This Power "resides within Intelligence, and without changing location; for the mind is not within any location, and Intelligence still less. Thus the soul is nowhere; she is a principle which, being nowhere, is everywhere." It is only after the individual mind has united with and become the Universal Mind that all kinds can be compacted "streight" within it; for the beam in its intellectual eye must first be removed and returned to the prime source of light. This is so, declares Plotinus, because "we possess the Ideas in a double manner; in the soul they appear developed and separate; in the Supreme Intelligence they exist all together." The Garden of Ideas is now contained in one Mind.

Then comes Marvell's magnificent climax, as surprising as it is inevitable.

> Yet it creates, transcending these,
> Far other Worlds, and other Seas;
> Annihilating all that's made
> To a green Thought in a green Shade.

In the last great couplet there is realized the figure of Leib- /24/ nitz's primary Monad—"Perceptive" in its symbolic representation of the whole poem, and "Appetitive" as well, since the whole cannot fulfill itself without it. Each word is cut by Marvell like facets of a crystal, through which shines the metaphorical light of the poem.

The thought is a "green Thought" because it is a thought *of* green, (the Garden of Ideas) and, since the Garden contains all thoughts, such a Thought must be the only Thought, the Thought of Thoughts, the Garden-Thought. The Shade is a "green Shade" because the "green Thought" enters it, becomes it, and stains it green, just as the mind enters into and becomes the Supreme Intelligence. As Aristotle said of his Prime Mover, (equal to Plotinus' Intellectual Principle), "since thought and the object of thought are not different in the case of things that have not matter, the divine thought and its object will be the same, i.e. the thinking will be one with the object of its thought." (*Meta.* 1074b-1075a) The Garden state is a state of mind.

Yet how can the Mind create a superflux of "other worlds and other seas" and, at the same time, annihilate "all that's made" to itself? The formo-logical and the theological roots of this paradox are intertwined. Considered formally, a concept of infinite extension which rises upon tier and tier of lesser concepts whose attributes it subsumes must, at last, possess no attributes of its own, contain everything and be nothing, of infinitesimal intention. Theologically, the Supreme Mind must have no envy of, nor deny actuality to, anything which exists potentially within it, or else suffer a diminution of itself; and contrarily, the Supreme Mind must also be self-contained and self-sufficient since it is of itself the divine Thought thinks and "its thinking is a thinking on thinking." In Marvell's triumphant solution of this paradox by fusing both terms of his metaphor in God, *his alchemical metaphor actually transmutes and transcends its /25/ own nature, only resembling what it has been before as A is A resembles a metaphorical identity.* Opus Operatum!

After the mind, the soul is likewise ready for transmigratory flight.

> Here at the Fountain's sliding foot,
> Or at some Fruit-trees mossy root,
> Casting the bodies vest aside
> My soul into the boughs does glide. . . .

The "sliding foot" of the Fountain and the "mossy root" of the fruit tree from which the soul glides off are substantially the same, since both are grounded in the twin sources of "The Garden"—Eden and the Realm of First Forms which Marvell identifies.

There was, of course the Tree of Life which grew in Paradise. But the real (i.e. metaphorical) source of the great Spring and the Tree is found in Plotinus.

> Imagine a spring that has no source outside itself; it gives itself to all the rivers, yet is never exhausted by what they take, but remains always integrally what it was; the tides that proceed from it are one within it before they run their several ways, yet all beforehand know down what channels they will pour their streams.
>
> Or:—think of the Life coursing through some mighty Tree while yet it is the stationary Principle of the whole, in no sense scattered over all that extent but, as it were, rested in the root; it is the giver of the entire and manifold life of the tree, but remains unmoved itself, not manifold but the Principle of that manifold life. (III, viii, 10)

In the tree, Marvell's soul assumes the dress of a bird.

> There like a bird it sits and sings
> Then whets, and combs its silver wings;
> And, till prepared for longer flight,
> Waves in its plumes the various light.

/26/ Such a reincarnation would be fitting for Marvell. According to Plotinus, "Those who have loved too much the enjoyments of music and who otherwise lived purely, pass into the bodies of melodious birds." (III, iv, 4) But until his bird-soul is ready for the "longer flight" to the One, it must bathe in the various light of the world. Plotinus considers this purgation an intermediate state for the soul when, in order to pass the time, "the body of the world comes to unite with her, and to offer the irradiation of its light." (III, iv, 4)

> Such was that happy Garden-state
> While Man there walked without a Mate;
> After a Place so pure, and sweet,
> What other Help could yet be meet!

It was the Garden of Eden before Eve came to spoil it, before the audacity of the soul degraded and multiplied itself.

> But 'twas beyond a Mortal's share
> To wander solitary there;
> Two Paradises 'twere in one
> To live in Paradise alone.

But only God can live alone in Paradise; for the Idea of the Garden, the substance of God, is the archetype for all other Paradises in men's minds. The last two lines, in their method and their meaning, recall the great couplet of the "green Shade." And yet—here is a curious thing—both couplets are related to one another as a copy is to the original, *as the "Mortal's share" of the Garden-thought is to the Idea in God's mind.* Marvell's poem is like a thinking mirror that reflects upon its own images.

Having already reached the outer margin of "The Garden," away from the burning center, Marvell reintroduces the discursive style of the opening stanza. /27/

> How well the skilful Gardner drew
> Of flow'rs and herbs this dial new;
> Where from above the milder sun
> Does through a fragrant Zodiac run;
> And, as it works, th' industrious Bee
> Computes its time as well as we. . . .

Time was created, thought Plotinus, as the moving image of eternity which was still and timeless. Its progress, however, can be measured by a dial formed by the "fragrant zodiac" of Plants, and its existence is coeval with the life of the soul.

> Thus the extension of the life of the soul produces time, and the perpetual progression of her life produces the perpetuity of time, and her former life constitutes the past. We may therefore properly define time as the life of the soul, considered in the movement by which she passes from one actualization to another. (III, vii, 10)

Under such a system the bee can "compute its time as well as we," since it is the same time for all things which exist under the sun.

But what an ironic nosegay this is with which to tie up the poem! For whoever have not acquired civil virtues in life (and the protagonist who yearned to "wander solitary there" is such a one), all these, says Plotinus, are "transformed into a sociable animal such as the bee, or other animal of the kind." (III, iv, 2) And here the poem ends.

> How could such sweet and wholesome Hours
> Be reckon'd but with Herbs and Flowers!

"The Garden" is now, I think, thoroughly cut and dried—and, despite all the hermeneutic rites and privileges of criticism, it may even be held a sacrilege by some, to have deflowered the metaphor. But such as it was it still remains, an imaginary Garden merely but with real Ideas in it. And all /28/ Gardens, the real and the unreal, must fade at last—Christ at his Nativity pillowed by straw from the withered Garden of Eden; and Marvell's Garden of First Forms, our universal, elemental hay, blooming only in the mind's eye.

Questions

Mr. Klonsky begins his essay by recognizing "The Garden" as a "version" of the pastoral. This essay was published in the same year as Ruth Wallerstein's book, and Klonsky's approach to the poem is similar to hers. Ruth Wallerstein restricts textual associations with "The Garden" to historical considerations; Klonsky further limits the process. The Neo-Platonic background for Marvell's poem is restricted to a single exponent, Plotinus. There is clearly, thus far, a continuity to the criticism on "The Garden." Conventions are being established for what is said about the poem, and how it is said.

> Mr. Klonsky speaks of "The Garden" as a poem with a periphery and a center. By comparing this essay with Ruth Wallerstein's, can you determine which parts (stanzas) of the poem are being singled out for special attention, and why?

Mr. Klonsky also considers "The Garden" as a poem with a plot and a main character. Who, in this essay, *is* your guide through the Garden?

After reading Wallerstein and Klonsky, what do you know about Plotinus? Do you thing Marvell might have read the *Enneads*? Is this consideration important?

Frank Kermode

The Argument of
Marvell's "Garden"*

I

'The Garden' is an *étude d'éxecution transcendante* which has
been interpreted by so many virtuosi in the past few years that a stiff-
fingered academic rendering is unlikely to be very entertaining.
However, since it appears that the brilliant executants have been
making rather too many mistakes, there may be some value in going
slowly over the whole piece.

It may be useful to point out in advance that these mistakes are of
three kinds. The first is historical, as when Mr. Milton Klonsky,
writing in the *Sewanee Review* (LVIII, 16-35), seizes on a passage in
Plotinus as the sole key to the poem. He is wrong, not because there
is no connection at all between Plotinus and Marvell's lyric, but be-
cause he has misunderstood the relationship and consequently exag-
gerated its importance. He fails to observe that Marvell, like other
poets of the period, uses philosophical concepts, including those of
Neo-Platonism, in a special way, with reference not to the body of
formal doctrine in which those concepts are originally announced,
but to genres of poetry which habitually and conventionally make
use of them. The process is familiar enough; for example, the nature
of the relationship between pastoral poetry and philosophic material
such as the debates on Action and Contemplation, Art and Nature, is
tolerably well understood. It is not customary to find the only key to
the works of Guarini or Fletcher in some Greek philosopher; but
these poets have not, like Donne and Marvell, been distorted by the
solemn enthusiasm of modern exegetes. In a sense all philosophical

*Reprinted from *Essays in Criticism*, II (July, 1952), 225-41, by permission of
the publisher and the author.

propositions in Marvell are what Professor Richards used to call 'pseudo-statements', and his is a 'physical' rather than a /226/ 'platonic' poetry. However, rather than risk myself in these deep waters, I shall support myself on a raft of Mr. Wellek's construction: 'The work of art . . . appears as an object *sui generis* . . . a system of norms of ideal concepts which are intersubjective . . .' Above all, it is possible 'to proceed to a classification of works of art according to the norms they employ' and thus 'we may finally arrive at theories of genres'.[1] The point is that we must not treat these 'norms' as propositions, for if we do we shall fall into the toils of Mr. Klonsky. Miss Ruth Wallerstein, who has worked so hard and so sanely to liberate seventeenth-century poetry from modern error, is none the less guilty of Mr. Klonsky's fault, in her *Studies in Seventeenth Century Poetic* (1950). Not only the indolent cry out against the suggestion that 'The Garden' needs to be explicated in terms of Hugo of St. Victor and Bonaventura. Doubtless there is, for the historian of ideas, a real connection between the poem and the Victorine and Neo-Platonic systems of symbolic thought; for there is a connection between Plato and 'Trees'. However interesting this may be, it has nothing to do with what most of us call criticism. If we read 'The Garden' as historians of poetry, and not as historians of ideas, we shall resist all such temptation to treat the 'norms' as ideas, even if it proceeds from Diotima herself, to whom Professor Richards succumbed in a recent lecture on the poem.

The second kind of mistake is one which, particularly when it assumes its more subtle shape, we are all liable to yield to, though it appears to be seductive even in its usual grossness. Sufficient, however, to say that 'The Garden' must not be read as autobiography. 'What was Marvell's state of mind as he wandered in Fairfax's Yorkshire garden?' is a very bad question to ask, but it is obviously one which comes readily to the minds of learned and subtle interpreters; both Marvell and Donne have suffered greatly from this form of misapplied scholarship, and it is comforting to reflect that the date of 'The Garden' is quite unknown, so that it cannot be positively stated to be the direct record of some personal experience at Nun Appleton. It could conceivably have been written much later. The /227/ pseudo-biographical critic is wasteful and deceptive; he diverts attention from the genre just as certainly as Mr. Klonsky does when he presents a picture of the poet torturing himself with Chinese boxes of Forms,

---

[1] 'The Mode of Existence of a Literary Work of Art,' *Critiques and Essays in Criticism, 1920-1948*, ed. R. W. Stallman, 1949, pp. 210-23.

or Mr. Empson when he invites us to reflect upon the Buddhist en-
lightenment (*Some Versions of Pastoral*, pp. 119-20).

The third kind of critical failure is clearly, in this case, the most
important, for the others would not have occurred had there not been
this cardinal error. It is the failure to appreciate the genre (the sys-
tem of 'norms' shared by other poems) to which 'The Garden' be-
longs. Despite the labours of Miss Bradbrook, Miss Lloyd Thomas,[2]
and Miss Wallerstein, poets like Théophile, Saint-Amant, Randolph,
Lovelace, Fane and Stanley have simply not been put to proper use
in the criticism of Marvell. This is the central difficulty, and the one
which this paper is intended to diminish. The first necessity is to
distinguish between the genre and the history of the ideas to which
the genre is related.

II

'We cannot erre in following Nature': thus Montaigne, 'very rawly
and simply', with this addition: 'I have not (as *Socrates*) by the
power and vertue of reason, corrected my natural complexions, nor
by Art hindered mine inclination."[3] This is a useful guide to that
aspect of 'naturalism' in the thought of the late Renaissance which
here concerns us. The like consideration governs all the speculations
of the older Montaigne; Nature is to be distinguished from Custom;
the natural inclinations are good, and sensual gratifications are not
the dangerous suggestions that other and more orthodox psychologies
hold them to be. Sense and instinct seek and find their own temper-
ance without the interference of reason. It is good to satisfy a natural
appetite, and it is also, of course, innocent. Thus men behaved, says
Montaigne, in the Golden World, and thus they still behave in the
Indies. /228/

The question how far Montaigne believed in his own 'primitivism'
seems to me a difficult one, but it scarcely concerns us at the moment.
It is legitimate to use him as spokesman for naturalism; and before
we leave him it will be prudent to glance at some of his references to
Plato, in order to have at hand some record of the naturalist reaction
to the Platonic theory of love. In short, as the foregoing quotation
implies, Platonic love is rejected. No longer 'an appetite of generation
by the mediation of beauty', love is in fact 'nothing else but an
insatiate thirst of enjoying a greedily desired subject' (III, 105). 'My

---

[2] M. C. Bradbrook, 'Marvell and the Poetry of Rural Solitude,' *RES* XVII
(1941), 37-46; M. C. BRADBROOK and M. G. LLOYD THOMAS, *Andrew Marvell*,
Cambridge, 1940.

[3] MONTAIGNE, *Essayes*, translated by John Florio, Everyman Edition, III, 316.

Page makes love, and understands it feelingly; Read *Leon Hebraeus*
or *Ficinus* unto him; you speake of him, of his thoughts and of his
actions, yet understands he nothing what you meane . . .' (III, 102).
Much more sympathetic are 'the ample and lively descriptions in
Plato, of the loves practised in his dayes' (III, 82). If one is not over-
careful—if, for instance, one fails to discriminate between the ora-
tions of Socrates and those who precede him, one may without much
difficulty extract from the *Symposium* itself very different theories of
love from those developed by Ficino or Milton. In Marvell's own
youth antithetical versions of Platonism flourished contemporane-
ously at Cambridge and at Whitehall.

So far we have concerned ourselves, very briefly, with the informal
naturalism of Montaigne, and hinted at a naturalistic version of
Plato. What of the poetry which concerns itself with similar issues?
One thinks at once of Tasso, and specifically of that chorus in his
Aminta, O bella età de l'oro, which was so often imitated and debated
in the poetry of the age. In the happy Golden Age lovers concerned
themselves with their own love and innocence, and not with honour,
that tyrant bred of custom and opinion, that enemy of nature. In the
garden of the unfallen just, whatever pleases is lawful. The paradise
of these fortunate innocents is abundant in its appeal to the senses;
law and appetite are the same, and no resolved soul interferes with
the banquet of sense offered by created pleasure. Thus an ancient
pastoral tradition accommodates new poetic motives, and poetry,
though affirming nothing, strengthens its association with the freer
thought of its time. The formal opposition of Tasso's statement is
properly made in poetry which belongs /229/ to the same genre; and
it may be found in the Chorus in Act IV of Guarini's *Il Pastor Fido*.
Parallel debates could go on in the great world, and in the little
world of poetry; the debate about naturalism was a serious one, since
it involved theological censures. The poetical debate is of a different
quality. The proper answer to Tasso is Guarini's. A genre of poetry
developed which assumed the right to describe the sensuality of a
natural Eden, and a specialized kind concentrated on sexual gratifica-
tions as innocent, and the subject of unreasonable interference from
Honour. The proper reply is, again, in terms of the 'norms' of the
genre, and there is evidence that the very poets who stated the ex-
treme naturalist case were quite capable of refuting it. One might call
the 'norms' of the refutation an anti-genre. 'The Garden' is a poem
of the anti-genre of the naturalist paradise.

Marvell therefore rejects the naturalist account of love, and with it
that Platonism which was associated with the delights of the senses.
The poets of the Renaissance were profitably aware of the possible

antitheses in Platonic theories of love, just as they were aware of
Plato's argument against their status as vessels of the truth.[4] Spenser
makes comfortable bedfellows of two Platonisms in his *Hymns*; the
two Aphrodites easily change into each other in poem and emblem.
Nothing is more characteristic of Renaissance poetry than the synthe-
sis of spiritual and erotic in poetic genre and image. It was encour-
aged by centuries of comment on the *Canticum Canticorum* and the
eclecticism of mystics as well as by the doctrinaire efforts of Bruno to
spiritualize the erotic Petrarcan conceits. Much more evidence could
be brought, if it were necessary, to establish the existence of genre
and anti-genre in Platonic love-poetry. They not only co-exist, but
suggest each other. Marvell could pass with ease from the libertine
garden to the garden of the Platonic *solitaire*, soliciting the primary
furor of spiritual ascent. (The ease of such transitions was partly
responsible for the development of another genre—that of the
palinode.) /230/

'The Garden' stands in relation to the poetry of the gardens of
sense as the *Hymn of Heavenly Beauty* stands in relation to the
Hymn of Beauty. It is poetry written in the language of, or using
the 'norms' of, a genre in a formal refutation of the genre. In fact,
this was a method Marvell habitually used, sometimes almost with an
affectation of pedantry, as I have elsewhere shown of 'The Mower
Against Gardens'.[5]

III

The garden is a rich emblem, and this is not the place to explore
it in any detail; indeed I shall say nothing of the symbolic gardens of
the Middle Ages which were still alive in the consciousness of the
seventeenth century. The gardens to which Marvell most directly
alludes in his poem are the Garden of Eden, the Earthly Paradise,
and that garden to which both Stoic and Epicurean, as well as Pla-
tonist, retire for solace or meditation. The first two are in many
respects one and the same; the third is the garden of Montaigne, of
Lipsius, and of Cowley. I shall not refer to the *hortus conclusus*,
though at one point in my explication of Marvell's poem I allude to
a Catholic emblem-writer. Doubtless the notion of Nature as God's

---

[4] See F. A. YATES, *The French Academies of the Sixteenth Century*, 1947, pp.
128ff. From Plato (*Symposium* 202A, *Republic* 477 *et seq.*) through the Pléiade to
Sidney there ran the argument that poets were not competent to make philosophical
statements; they affirm nothing.

[5] *Notes and Queries*, March 29th, 1952, pp. 136-8.

book affects the poetic tradition; it certainly occurs in poems about solitude at this period. But I think it is misleading to dwell on the history of the idea.

Of the complexity of the Earthly Paradise, with all its associated images and ideas, it is not necessary to say much: it is of course a staple of pastoral poetry and drama, and the quality of Marvell's allusions to it will emerge in my explication. But a word is needed about the garden of the solitary thinker, which Marvell uses in his argument against the libertine garden of innocent sexuality.

It is to be remembered that we are not dealing with the innocence of Tasso's Golden Age, where there is a perfect concord between appetite and reason, or with the garden of innocent love that Spenser sketches in *Faerie Queene*, IV, x, where 'thousand payres of louers walkt, Praysing their god, and yeelding him great thankes', and 'did sport Their spotlesse /231/ pleasures, and sweet loues content'. The libertines use the argument of the innocence of sense to exalt sensuality and to propose the abolition of the tyrant Honour, meaning merely female chastity. This is the situation of the *Jouissance* poetry which was fashionable in France, and of which Saint-Amant's well-known example, excellently translated by Stanley, is typical. It is equally the situation of Randolph's 'Upon Love Fondly Refused' and his 'Pastoral Courtship', Carew's 'Rapture' and Lovelace's 'Love Made in the first Age'. In Randolph's Paradise there is no serpent—'Nothing that wears a sting, but I'[6]—and in Lovelace's

> No Serpent kiss poyson'd the Tast
> Each touch was naturally Chast,
> And their mere Sense a Miracle.[7]

And so it is throughout the libertine versions of sensual innocence. The garden, the place of unfallen innocence, is identified with a naturalist glorification of sensuality. The garden which is formally opposed to this one by Marvell is the garden where sense is controlled by reason and the intellect can contemplate not beauty but heavenly beauty.

It was Montaigne, this time in his Stoic role, who gave wide currency to the pleasures of *solitary* seclusion. The relevant ideas and attitudes were developed into a poetic genre. Many poets certainly known to Marvell practised this genre, among them Fane and Fairfax and the French poets, notably Saint-Amant, whose *Solitude* demon-

---

[6] *Poems,* ed. G. Thorn-Drury, 1929, p. 110.
[7] *Poems,* ed. C. H. Wilkinson, 1930, p. 147.

strates how easily he moved in this, the antithesis of the *Jouissance*
mode. This famous poem was translated by Fairfax and by Katharine
Phillips. This is the poetry of the meditative garden, whether the
meditation be pseudo-Dionysian, or Ciceronian, or merely pleasantly
Epicurean, like Cowley's. There is, of course, a play of the senses in
which woman has no necessary part, though the equation of all
appetite with the sexual appetite in the libertines tends to ignore it;
this unamorous sensuality is firmly castigated by Lipsius in his treat-
ment of gardens. If the garden is /232/ treated merely as a resort of
pleasure, for the 'inward tickling and delight of the senses' it becomes
'a verie sepulchre of slothfulnes'. The true end of the garden is
'quietnes, withdrawing from the world, meditation', the subjection
of the distressed mind to right reason.[8] The true ecstasy is in being
rapt by intellect, not by sex.

Retirement; the study of right reason; the denial of the sovereignty
of sense; the proper use of created nature: these are the themes of
Marvell's poem laboriously and misleadingly translated into prose.
As poetry the work can only be studied in relation to its genre,
though that genre may be related to ethical debates. To the naturalist
Jouissance Marvell opposes the meditative *Solitude*. The fact that
both these opposed conceptions are treated in the work of one poet,
Saint-Amant, and a little less explicitly in Théophile and Randolph
also, should warn against the mistaking of seriousness for directness
of reference to ethical propositions. 'The Garden' uses and revalues
the 'norms' of the genre: it is not a contribution to philosophy, and
not the direct account of a contemplative act.

IV

Henry Hawkins, the author of the emblem-book *Partheneia Sacra*,
adopts a plan which enables him, in treating the emblematic qualities
of a garden, to direct the attention of the pious reader away from
the delights of the sense offered by the plants to a consideration
of their higher significance. As in Marvell, sensual pleasure has to
give way to meditation.[9] We now proceed to the explication of Mar-
vell's poem, with a glance at Hawkins's wise disclaimer: 'I will not
take upon me to tel al; for so of a Garden of flowers, should I make
a Labyrinth of discourse, and should never be able to get forth' (p. 8).

The poem begins by establishing that of all the possible gardens it

---

[8] *De Constantia, Of Constancie,* translated by Sir J. Stradling, ed. R. Kirk and
C. M. Hall, 1939, pp. 132ff.

[9] *Partheneia Sacra,* ed. Iain Fletcher, 1950 (reprint of 1633), p. 2.

is dealing with that of retirement, with the garden of the contemplative man who shuns action. The retired life is preferred to the active life in a witty simplification: if the two ways of life are appraised in terms of the vegetable solace they /233/ provide it will be seen that the retired life is quantitatively superior. The joke is in the substitution of the emblem of victory for its substance. If you then appraise action in terms of plants you get single plants, whereas retirement offers you the solace of not one but *all* plants. This is a typical 'metaphysical' use of the figure called by Puttenham the Disabler. The first stanza, then, is a witty dispraise of the active life, though it has nothing to distinguish it sharply from other kinds of garden-poetry such as libertine or Epicurean—except possibly the hint of a secondary meaning 'celibate' in the word *single* and a parallel sexual pun on *close*,[10] which go very well with the leading idea that woman has no place in this garden.

The Innocence of the second stanza cannot itself divide the poem from other garden-poems; for Innocence of a sort is a feature of the libertine paradise, as well as of the Epicurean garden of Cowley and indeed most gardens.

> Your sacred Plants, if here below,
> Only among the Plants will grow—

lines which are certainly a much more complicated statement than that of *Hortus*—seem to have stimulated Mr. Klonsky to astonishing feats. But the idea is not as difficult as all that. Compare 'Upon Appleton House'—

> For he did, with his utmost Skill,
> *Ambition* weed, but *Conscience* till,
> *Conscience,* that Heaven-nursed Plant,
> Which most our Earthly Gardens want. (XLV)

Your sacred plants, he says, addressing Quiet and Innocence, are unlike the palm, the oak and the bays in that if you find them anywhere on earth it will be among the plants of the garden. The others you can find 'in busie Companies'. The joke here is to give Quiet and her sister plant-emblems like those of the active life, and to clash the emblematic and the vegetable plants together. The inference is that Innocence may be found only in the green shade (*concolor Umbra*

---

[10] Proposed by A. H. KING, *English Studies*, XX (1938), 118-21.

occurs at this point in /234/ the Latin version). Society (with its ordinary connotations of 'polish' and 'company') is in fact all but rude (unpolished) by comparison with Solitude, which at first appears to be lacking in the virtues Society possesses, but which possesses them, if the truth were known, in greater measure (the Ciceronian-Stoic 'never less alone than when alone' became so trite that Cowley, in his essay 'Of Solitude', apologized for referring to it).

We are now ready for a clearer rejection of libertine innocence. Female beauty is reduced to its emblematic colours, red and white (a commonplace, but incidentally one found in the libertine poets) and unfavourably compared with the green of the garden as a dispenser of sensual delight. This is to reject Saint-Amant's 'crime innocent, à quoi la Nature consent'.[11] A foolish failure to understand the superiority of green causes lovers to insult trees (themselves the worthier objects of love) by carving on them the names of women. (This happens in Saint-Amant's *Jouissance.*) Since it is the green garden, and not women that the poet chooses to regard as amorous, it would be farcically logical for him to carve on the trees their own names. The garden is not to have women or their names or their love in it. It is natural (green) and amorous (green—a 'norm' of the poem) in quite a different way from the libertine garden.

Love enters this garden, but only when the pursuit of the white and red is done, and we are without appetite. (Love is here indiscriminately the pursued and the pursuer. Weary with the race and exertion (*heat*) it 'makes a retreat' in the garden; hard-pressed by pursuers it carries out a military retreat.) The place of retreat has therefore Love, but not women: they are metamorphosed into trees. The gods, who might be expected to know, have been misunderstood; they pursued women not as women but as potential trees, for the green and not for the red and white. Marvell, in this witty version of the metamorphoses, continues to 'disable' the idea of sexual love. Here one needs quite firmly to delimit the reference, because it is confusing to think of *laurel* and *reed* as having symbolic significations. It is interesting that this comic metamorphosis (which has affinities with the fashionable mock-heroic) was /235/ practised for their own ends by the libertine poets; for example, in Saint-Amant's 'La Metamorphose de Lyrian et de Sylvie', in Stanley's Marinesque 'Apollo and Daphne', in Carew's 'Rapture', where Lucrece and other types of chastity become sensualists in the libertine paradise, and very notably in Lovelace. Thus, in 'Against the Love of Great Ones':

---

[11] *Œuvres Complètes*, ed. Ch.-L. Livet, 1855, I, 119.

> *Ixion* willingly doth feele
> The Gyre of his eternal wheele,
> Nor would he now exchange his paine
> For Cloudes and Goddesses againe. (*Poems,* p. 75)

The sensuous appeal of this garden is, then, not sexual, as it is in the libertines. It has, none the less, all the enchantment of the Earthly Paradise, and all its innocence: this is the topic of the fifth stanza. The trees and plants press their fruit upon him, and their gifts are in strong contrast to those of the libertine garden,

> Love then unstinted, Love did sip,
> And Cherries pluck'd fresh from the Lip,
>   On Cheeks and Roses free he fed;
> Lasses like *Autumne* Plums did drop,
> And Lads, indifferently did crop
>   A Flower, and a Maiden-head. (*Poems,* p. 146)

The fruits of green, not of red and white, are offered in primeval abundance, as they are in the Fortunate Islands or in any paradise. Everything is by nature lush and fertile; the difference between this and a paradise containing a woman is that here a Fall is of light consequence, and without tragic significance. ('Insnar'd with *flowers, I* fall on grass.') In the same way, Marvell had in 'Upon Appleton House' (LXXVII) bound himself with the entanglements not of wanton limbs, in the libertine manner of Carew, Randolph and Stanley, but of woodbine, briar and bramble. The same imagery is still in use for amorous purposes in the poetry of Leigh.

In this garden both man and nature are unfallen; it is therefore, for all its richness, not a trap for virtue but a paradise of /236/ perfect innocence. Even the fall is innocent; the sensuous allurements of the trees are harmless, and there is no need to 'fence The Batteries of alluring Sense'. It is evident that Empson and King were quite right to find here a direct allusion to the Fall.

Modern commentators all agree that the sixth stanza, central to the poem, is a witty Platonism, and of course this is so. The danger is that the Platonism can be made to appear doctrinal and even recherché, when in fact it is reasonably modest, and directly related to genre treatments of love in gardens. There is, however, a famous ambiguity in the first two lines: how are we to take 'from pleasure less'? It can mean simply (1) reduced by pleasure, or (2) that the mind retires because it experiences less pleasure than the senses, or (3) that it retires from the lesser pleasure to the greater. The first of these might be related to the doctrine of the creation in *Paradise Lost*, VII, 168f.—'I am who fill Infinitude, nor vacuous the space. Though I uncircumscrib'd myself retire, And put not forth my goodness . . .' This would be consistent with the analogy later drawn between the human and the divine minds. But the second is more likely to be the dominant meaning, with a proper distinction between mind and sense which is obviously relevant to the theme ('None can chain a mind Whom this sweet Chordage cannot bind'). The third meaning is easily associated with this interpretation. The mind withdraws from the sensual gratification offered in order to enjoy a happiness of the imagination. In terms of the genre, it rejects the *Jouissance* for the *Solitude*—indeed, Saint-Amant, in a poem which prefers the contemplative garden, writes of it thus:

> Tantost, faisant agir mes sens
> Sur des sujets *de moindre estofe,*
> De marche en autre je descens
> Dans les termes du philosophe;
> Nature n'a point de secret
> Que d'un soin libre, mais discret,
> Ma curiosité ne sonde;
> Et, dans ma recherche profonde,
> Je loge en moy tout l'univers. /237/
> Là, songeant au flus et reflus,
> *Je m'abisme dans cette idée;*
> Son mouvement me rend perclus,
> Et mon âme en est obsedée. (I, 32; my italics)

To put it another way, one prefers a different kind of ecstasy from that of the libertine, described by the same poet in his *Jouissance*, which Stanley translated. Saint-Amant represents his solitary as acquiring from nature knowledge of the forms, and the next two lines of Marvell's stanza seem to do likewise. The metaphor is not unfamiliar—'Some have affirm'd that what on earth we find The sea can parallel for shape and kind'—and the idea is that the forms exist in the mind of man as they do in the mind of God. By virtue of the imagination the mind can create worlds and seas too which have nothing to do with the world which is reported by the senses. This is the passage which seems to have caused such trouble to commentators, who look to learned originals like Plotinus and Ficino for the explanation: but in fact the Platonism here is dilute and current.

It is a commonplace of Renaissance poetic that God is a poet, and that the poet has the honour of this comparison only because of the

creative force of fancy or imagination. Nor is the power exclusive to
poets. The mind, which 'all effects into their causes brings'[12] can
through the imagination alone devise new and rare things: as Put-
tenham says, 'the phantasticall part of man (if it be not disordered)
is a representer of the best, most comely and bewtifull images or ap-
parences of thinges to the soule and according to their very truth'
(p. 19). Puttenham shuns 'disordered phantasies . . . monstruous
imaginations or conceits' as being alien to the truth of imagination,
but it is conceivable that Marvell, in his suggestion of the mind's
ability to create, refers to a more modern psychology and poetic,
with its roots in the Renaissance, but with a new emphasis. Thus
Cowley in his Pindaric 'The Muse' says that the coach of poetry can
go anywhere: /238/

> And all's an *open Road* to *thee.*
> Whatever *God* did say,
> Is all thy plain and smooth, uninterrupted *Way.*
> Nay, ev'n beyond his *Works* thy *Voyages* are known,
> Thou hast a thousand *Worlds* too of thine *own.*
> Thou speak'st, great *Queen*, in the same *Stile* as *he,*
> And *a new World* leaps forth, when *thou* say'st, *Let it be.*

And in a note he obligingly explains this:

> The meaning is, that *Poetry* treats not only of all Things that are, or can
> be, but makes *Creatures* of her own, as *Centaurs, Satyrs, Fairies,* &c.,
> makes *Persons* and *Actions* of her own . . . makes *Beasts, Trees, Waters,*
> and other irrational and insensible Things to act above the Possibility
> of their Natures as to *understand* and *speak*; nay makes what *Gods* it
> pleases too without *Idolatry*, and varies all these into innumerable
> *Systemes*, or *Worlds* of Invention.

These other worlds are thoughts in the mind of man as the world
is a thought in the mind of God. Empson is probably right in his
guess that *streight* means 'packed together' as well as 'at once'. The
whole idea is illuminated by a passage of extraordinary interest in
Leigh (who was imbued with that passion for optics which later
became common among poets) in which the reduced images of the
eye are contrasted with the illimitable visions of the mind. The mind
contains everything undiminished by the deficiencies of sense.[13] The

---

[12] SIR JOHN DAVIES, *Nosce Teipsum* ('The Intellectual Powers of the Soul',
stanza 5).

[13] *Poems*, ed. Hugh Macdonald, 1947, pp. 36ff.

mental activity which Marvell is describing is clear; it is the working
of the imagination, which, psychologically, follows sense and pre-
cedes intellection, and is therefore the means of rejecting the volup-
tuous suggestions of sense; and which 'performs its function when
the sensible object is rejected or even removed'.[14] The mind's newly
created worlds are, in the strict sense, phantasms, and without sub-
stance: and since they have the same mental status as the created
world, it is fair to say that 'all that's made' is being annihilated,
reduced to a thought. /239/

But a green thought? This is a great bogey; but surely the thought
is green because the solitude is green, which means that it is also
the antithesis of voluptuousness? Here the normative signification of
green in the poem is in accord with what is after all a common
enough notion—green for innocence, Thus, in 'Aramantha' Lovelace
asks:

> Can trees be green, and to the Ay'r
> Thus prostitute their flowing Hayr? (*Poems*, p. 112)

But I cannot think the green has any more extensive symbolic
intention. Green is still opposed to red and white; all this is possible
only when women are absent and the senses innocently engaged.

The stanza thus alludes to the favourable conditions which enable
the mind to apply itself to contemplation. The process is wittily
described, and the psychology requires no explanation in terms of
any doctrinaire Platonism, whether pseudo-Dionysian, Plotinian, or
Florentine.

The seventh stanza is also subject to much ingenious comment.
The poet allows his mind to contemplate the ideas, and his soul
begins a Platonic ascent. Here there are obvious parallels in the
English mystics, in Plotinus, in medieval and Florentine Platonism;
but we must see this stanza as we see the rest of the poem, in rela-
tion to the genre. Failing to do this we shall be involved in an end-
less strife between rival symbolisms, as we are if we try to find an
external significance for *green*. As it is, there is no need to be
over-curious about the fountain; its obvious symbolic quality may
have an interesting history, but it is primarily an easily accessible
emblem of purity. As for the use of the bird as an emblem of the
soul, that is an image popularized by Castiglione,[15] and used by
Spenser of the early stages of the ascent:

---

[14] Gianfrancesco Pico della Mirandola, *De Imaginatione*, edited and translated
by H. Caplan, 1930, p. 29.

[15] *The Book of the Courtier*, translated by Thomas Hoby, Everyman Edition,
p. 338.

Beginning then below, with th'easie vew
Of this base world, subiect to fleshly eye,
From thence to mount aloft by order dew,
To contemplation of th'immortall sky,
Of that soare faulcon so I learne to fly, /240/
That flags awhile her fluttering wings beneath,
Till she her selfe for stronger flight can breath.

(*Hymne of Heavenly Beauty*, pp. 22-8)

Spenser has just passed from the consideration of woman's love and beauty to the heavenly love and beauty. The bird which prepares its wings for flight is evidently a symbol with as settled a meaning as the dew, which Marvell also shared with many other poets.

The hungry soul, deceived with false beauties, may have 'after vain deceiptfull shadowes sought'—but at last it looks 'up to that soveraine light, From whose pure beams al perfect beauty springs' (*H.H.B.*, 291, 295). Marvell's bird 'Waves in its Plumes the various Light.' Once more we might spring to Ebreo or Plotinus or even Haydocke, but we shall do better to note how this same image is used in literature more closely related to Marvell.

Les oyseaux, d'un joyeux ramage,
En chantant semblent adorer
La lumière qui vient dorer
Leur cabinet et leur plumage—

thus Théophile, in his Ode, 'Le Matin'.[16] In *Partheneia Sacra* Hawkins uses the dove as other poets use the dew or the rainbow—

Being of what coulour soever, her neck being opposed to the Sun wil diversify into a thousand coulours, more various than the Iris it-self, or that Bird of *Juno* in al her pride; as scarlet, cerulean, flame-coulour, and yealding a flash like the Carbuncle, with vermilion, ash-coulour, and manie others besides. . . . (p. 202)

Marvell's use of the Platonic light-symbolism is therefore not technical, as it might be in Chapman, but generalized, as in Quarles or Vaughan, and affected by imagery associated with the garden genres. We are thus reminded that the point about the ascent towards the pure source of light is not that it can be achieved, but that it can be a product of *Solitude* rather than /241/ of *Jouissance* and that it is an alternative to libertine behaviour in gardens. It is the ecstasy not of beauty but of heavenly beauty.

---

[16] *Œuvres Complètes*, ed. M. Alleaume, 1856, I, 174-5.

The eighth stanza at last makes this theme explicit. This is a special solitude, which can only exist in the absence of women, the agents of the most powerful voluptuous temptation. This has been implied throughout, but it is now wittily stated in the first clear reference to Eden. The notion that Adam would have been happy without a mate is not, of course, novel; St. Ambrose believed it. Here it is another way of putting the case that woman offers the wrong beauty, the wrong love, the red and white instead of the green. Eve deprived Adam of solitude, and gave him instead an inferior joy. Indeed she was his punishment for being mortal (rather than pure Intelligence?). Her absence would be equivalent to the gift of a paradise (since her presence means the loss of the only one there is). This is easy enough, and a good example of how naturally we read references to the more familiar conceptions of theology and philosophy as part of the play of wit within the limited range of a genre.

In the last stanza the temperate quiet of the garden is once more asserted, by way of conclusion. (The Earthly Paradise is always in the temperate zone.) The time, for us as for the bee (a pun on 'thyme') is sweet and rewarding; hours of innocence are told by a dial of pure herbs and flowers. The sun is 'milder' because in this zodiac of flowers fragrance is substituted for heat; Miss Bradbrook and Miss Lloyd Thomas have some good observations here. The time computed is likewise spent in fragrant rather than hot pursuits. This is the *Solitude*, not the *Jouissance*; the garden of the *solitaire* whose soul rises towards divine beauty, not that of the voluptuary who voluntarily surrenders to the delights of the senses.

This ends the attempt to read 'The Garden' as a poem of a definite historical kind and to explore its delicate allusions to a genre of which the 'norms' are within limits ascertainable. Although it is very improbable that such an attempt can avoid errors of both sophistication and simplification, one may reasonably claim for it that in substituting poetry for metaphysics it does no violence to the richness and subtlety of its subject.

Questions

Frank Kermode's essay changes the tone of the criticism on Marvell's poem. Mr. Kermode also attempts to change the direction of our efforts to understand this poem. If certain norms are being established for our thinking on "The Garden," they are in Kermode's opinion the wrong ones. "If we read 'The Garden' as historians of poetry, and not as historians of ideas, we shall resist all such temptation to treat the 'norms' as ideas, even if it proceeds from Diotima herself . . ." Kermode proposes a clear explanation of the literary system of norms, or "genre," to which "The Garden" belongs.

In Part I of his essay, Mr. Kermode criticizes Empson, Wallerstein and Klonsky. Do you accept the terms of this criticism?

What is the purpose of Part II? Is Montaigne a better "guide through the Garden" than Plotinus?

What is the importance of the word "jouissance" to Kermode's argument?

In the last sentence of his article, Mr. Kermode states that his reading of "The Garden" substitutes "poetry" for "metaphysics." Is this an accurate estimation of the essay? What is the genre to which "The Garden" belongs, or against which it reacts? Is this genre historically verified?

Pierre Legouis

Marvell and the New Critics*[1]

When our secretary asked me to read a paper before this confer-
ence it was suggested that the title might run: 'Second thoughts on
Marvell.' But upon examination the dreadful reality revealed itself
starkly to me: I had *no* second thoughts on Marvell, at least not on
his poetry. Since my bulky book came out in 1928 I have had to
revise my views on his wife, or rather non-wife. And by discovering
his presence at Saumur in 1656 Mrs. Duncan-Jones has opened to me
new vistas on the religious thought of his later years. As an historian
I should have liked to give you today a picture of that small French
town, then at the height of its intellectual fame. But this could
hardly have led to a discussion, and discussion is what the organizers
of the conference are after. Do not blame *me* then if this paper
adopts a provocative, nay an aggressive, tone and roundly attacks all
those who have presumed, in the last twenty-eight years, to discover
new meanings in Marvell's poems. For I shall use the term 'new
criticism' in a very inclusive sense, regardless of the division of
opinion between schools or coteries, English and American, even con-
founding Cantabs with Oxonians. Whether they like it or not, to an
impartial and sufficiently remote observer they all derive from Pro-
fessor Empson's *Seven Types of Ambiguity* (1930). Further than
that in their pedigree I will not go. The philosophical and psycho-
logical basis for their method I shall ignore. Were I a blunt English-

Reprinted from *Review of English Studies,* n.s. VIII (November, 1957), 382-89,
by permission of the Clarendon Press, Oxford, and the author. Only pages 382-87
are reprinted in this volume.

[1] This paper was read at the Third Triennial Conference of the International
Association of University Professors of English at Cambridge in August 1956. It
has been left practically unaltered.

man I should say I neither know nor care whence it originates. By their fruit I will know them. Have they brought forth any interpretation, both new and valid, of any poem, stanza, or line?

Though in his afore-mentioned book Mr. Empson discussed several poems of Marvell's and performed some remarkable feats with them, his main contribution to the Marvellian new look is the article on 'The Garden' published in *Scrutiny*, i (1932). Indeed 'The Garden' has since been the most frequently re-examined of Marvell's poems; and, my time being limited, I shall concentrate on it almost exclusively.

Here is a sample of Mr. Empson's method. Stanza vi, as you know, opens:

> Meanwhile the Mind, from pleasure less,
> Withdraws into its happiness; /383/

From pleasure less. Either 'from the lessening of pleasure . . .' or 'made less by pleasure . . .'. Since three meanings, in Mr. Empson's theory, are better than two, his omission of the real meaning conclusively shows that he never saw it: 'from a pleasure that is inferior' (see *O.E.D.* under *Less*, 2), viz. sensuous pleasure, the mind withdraws into a happiness that is specifically its own, viz. contemplation. Here Mr. Empson does exactly what many a bright student has been doing for the last thirty-four years in translations set by me: not seeing the obvious meaning of a phrase and seeing entirely improbable ones instead, *gallice* 'faire un contre-sens.' So that, to parody a regal remark, we are amused, but we are not impressed.

However, Mr. Empson does not stop *en si beau chemin*, but proceeds with the next couplet:

> The mind that Ocean where each kind
> Does streight its own resemblance find;

Here my friend Margoliouth's standard edition provides him with the true meaning, in the form of a quotation from *Pseudodoxia Epidemica*, to which I have added one from Butler and this from Cleveland:

> Some have affirm'd that what on earth we find
> The sea can parallel for shape and kind.

But, in order to form one of his beloved dyads, Mr. Empson remarks that the sea also is a conscious mirror, and 'if calm reflects everything'. I answer, with gross literalness, that the sea will not reflect 'each kind' (of animals or plants) unless you previously hang them above it, a process involving even more difficulties than Noah was faced with when called upon to build the Ark. Such a vagary as Mr. Empson's, forgivable only in a reader reduced to his twentieth-century knowledge, or ignorance, of natural history, is here positively harmful, since it distracts the mind (our mind) from the historical meaning, the only one that Marvell meant, the obvious one for mid-seventeenth-century men.

It was to be expected that a religious and a sexual ambiguity, or a religiously-sexual, or a sexually-religious, ambiguity should be extracted from some part of the poem. The stanza selected for this treatment is the fifth, and especially its final couplet:

> Stumbling on Melons, as I pass,
> Insnared with Flow'rs, I fall on grass.

Mr. Empson wonders whether admiring readers 'have recognized that the A and Ω of the stanza are the Apple and the Fall', since 'Melon . . . is Greek for apple'. Indeed *I* had not. Nor had I noticed that the stanza 'is the triumph of Marvell's attempt to impose a sexual interest upon Nature'. I had fondly imagined, so far, that the poet had left, for a time at least, the /384/ 'sexual interest' behind him, in London Cavalier society, and explicitly sacrificed women to trees in stanzas iii and iv. But now I am quite prepared to reconsider these 'Melons' in a new light. Only I must ask myself why Marvell also placed them (erroneously or not) on the soil of the Bermudas: is it to 'ensnare' the Greekless Puritan emigrants who foolishly thank God for them? He 'throws the Melons at our feet'. Indeed I wonder why nobody has yet (to my knowledge) given a psychoanalytic explanation of these 'melons': in Greek they are apples, Mr. Empson reminds us, and in French 'pommes' is sometimes applied, in a very informal style, to those globular charms that have made Marilyn Monroe and Gina Lollobrigida famous in our time. As a result no doubt of repression, the English Puritans, probably in a dream, find these instruments of the Fall of Man enticing them to 'fall on grass'.

If you say I exaggerate I shall refer you to the next full-scale commentary on 'The Garden', a much ampler one than Mr. Empson's. Mr. Milton Klonsky apparently has a full right to the title of 'new critic', since his article 'A Guide through *The Garden*' appeared in the *Sewanee Review*, lviii (1950). He adopts a good many interpretations from Mr. Empson, particularly that of the melons being the forbidden fruit, and Marvell's fall on the grass 'a corruptive action'.

The 'ripe round feminine forms' are, moreover, recognized, not only in the Greek melons and the English apples, but also in the peaches (possibly with an anticipation of the American 'she is a peach'), the nectarines, and even the grape. As an inevitable consequence 'the sensuality which had been steadily rising up to now is climactically discharged', whatever this may mean.

But Mr. Klonsky's article is not all fun. He has warned us in his preamble that the poem could be thoroughly understood only through the study of Plotinus' *Enneads*. I have no *a priori* objection to such an approach, provided the obvious sense of the poem suffers no distortion, but this is just what befalls it here. Mr. Klonsky wants to prove that Marvell—or Marvell's 'protagonist' as he curiously calls him—is guilty of 'sensuality', and he punishes, or cures, him with death, the result of which appears in stanza vi, already quoted. Now, says Mr. Klonsky, 'the soul and the body are dissevered'. They are, in a way, since the mind cuts itself off from sensation, but why obtrude death here? And, what is even worse, why introduce an idea of guilt where the poem gives a happy gradation from the inferior (less) but quite legitimate pleasure of a vegetable life, to the higher pleasure of contemplation, itself only a step to the ecstasy in the next stanza? Mr. Klonsky's introduction of guilt is, to use his own phrase, 'a corruptive action'.

I must now go back a dozen years or so and say a word of the useful 'Notes' on 'The Garden' contributed by Mr. A. H. King to *English Studies* /385/ in 1938. But should he rank among the new critics except in point of date? His careful examination of the English text in connexion with the Latin one satisfies the rules of caution laid down by the old criticism at almost every point. If he refers to Mr. Empson's Apple-and-Fall interpretation he tones it down considerably. On the other hand I agree with him that in 'The Garden' Marvell's 'approach should be kept distinct from the mortally earnest approach to Nature of a Romantic poet like Shelley' (indeed I had said so in my book)—but I disagree with the epithet 'mincing' applied by Mr. King to Marvell's 'approach': as if there were no other choice than that between Romanticism and effeminacy. I should rather say that the Romantic poets lack a certain form of *pudor*, which Marvell has, while he can be serious enough under the surface. And against Mr. King's restrictive criticism of 'a green thought in a green shade' I must protest, because he takes up a remark of mine (in a footnote) that 'green' can mean 'naïve' and regrets my 'building nothing on this'. I shall retort that *he* builds more than the remark will bear, for, as I had been careful to say, the usual senses of green,

including this one, prove inadequate here, and there is mystery in
the phrase.

An even more detailed study than Mr. Klonsky's followed closely.
It was no less 'new' since it appeared in *Essays in Criticism*, ii (1952).
It bears the title 'The Argument of Marvell's *Garden*'. With its
author, Mr. Frank Kermode, I often agree, all the more readily since
he rather confirms (tacitly) than contradicts what I had said of yore.
If I have a complaint against him, it is that he goes too far in the
right direction, e.g. when he dismisses autobiographical interpreta-
tion. Attention paid to the genre, however profitable, does not con-
stitute the sum total of criticism, and Mr. Kermode rather overworks
the notion. The terms 'genre' and 'species' are relative, as we learnt at
school; but while the seventeenth century acknowledged the pastoral
as a genre it would not have recognized the genre of 'garden poetry' as
defined by Mr. Kermode. Even today the more modest term 'theme'
might prove more suitable here.

Anyhow, in the so-called genre, poems by Théophile and Saint-
Amant are included. Of course, as early as 1930, Mr. Geoffrey Woledge
had called attention to them in connexion with Lord Fairfax and his
daughter's tutor, and had said they were in the same 'tradition'. Miss
Bradbrook, in 1941, had considerably enlarged the claim on behalf
of the French *libertins*, and Miss Ruth Wallerstein had followed suit
in 1950. These three critics had chiefly stressed the literary resem-
blances between Marvell and his French predecessors. I must say I
remained somewhat sceptical, because when preparing my book I had
read these poets and been struck more by the differences, still literary,
between them and Marvell, who, by the way, could not scan a French
line though he could read French prose easily /386/ enough. But I
would not refuse the honour paid to my country and kept silent. Now
Mr. Kermode, curtly dismissing his English or American predecessors,
stresses the sufficiently obvious moral differences between Marvell
and Saint-Amant or Théophile, and sets out to prove that Marvell
wrote to contradict, or to refute, them in the same style. Mr. Kermode
even erects 'The Garden' into an 'anti-genre'. Here I must come in
and, paradoxically for a Frenchman, accuse an Englishman of too
systematic a treatment of the problem. There is little polemical spirit
in 'The Garden'. The only satiric touch, the word 'fond' applied to
male lovers, denotes smiling intellectual superiority rather than
moral reprobation. Neither are the ladies at all severely handled:
their 'white or red' (natural it seems) is indeed placed lower than the
'lovely green' of the plants, but, as the Latin version testifies, Marvell
grants them a very moving beauty: 'Vergineae quem non suspendit

gratia formae?' They surpass the snow in whiteness and the purple in redness—only the green stands in a class by itself. But here again Mr. Kermode reacts against his predecessors—except Mr. King—this time by denying that there is anything special in this word 'green'. He calls the 'green thought' the 'great bogey'. This seems to me to be carrying to excess the reaction against such philosophizing and scholasticizing of the epithet as Miss Wallerstein's. Certainly the thought is green because the solitude is green, but does it really end there?

To prove that he is a 'new critic' *stricto sensu* in spite of his fondness for genre, Mr. Kermode pronounces it evident that Empson and King were right to find in stanza v 'a direct allusion to the Fall' and dilates on the 'famous ambiguity' in the beginning of stanza vi: 'from pleasure less'. He indeed admits the only sensible interpretation (omitted by Mr. Empson) but he does so in a half-hearted and shamefaced manner. Yet his conclusion on the passage tallies with mine: 'the Platonism is here dilute and current'. I had spoken, apropos of 'A Drop of Dew', but with general application to Marvell's poetry, of 'platonisme diffus'. However, when he comes to stanza vii, Mr. Kermode, still in virtue of his system, unduly lessens Marvell's originality. To the lines

> Casting the bodies vest aside
> My soul into the boughs does glide:
> There like a Bird it sits and sings,

he discovers many parallels. But they entirely fail—in particular those culled by him in Saint-Amant and Théophile fail—to give the impression of the poet's identification with Nature that Marvell's metaphor gives, and here resides the unique value of that moment. For, while no one could deny the allusion to heaven in the last line but one, 'till prepared for longer flight', it sounds rather perfunctory. Marvell certainly wants to go to a still /387/ better place some day, but no less certainly he does not want to go yet. He is fully satisfied with a condition very similar to that described in a famous passage of 'Upon Appleton House', where he talks with the birds 'in their most learned original'. His past belongs to Woman, his future to God, but his present belongs to Nature alone. And at the risk of shocking religious souls, I consider that the premature intrusion of God into Mr. Kermode's commentary spoils the instant. Truth to say, Marvell himself does not remain thus poised, and the next stanza, the eighth, cannot but come as an anticlimax with its reference—a playful one—

to the earthly Paradise. Yet, says Mr. Kermode, it clinches the 'Argument'; here Marvell 'at last makes [his] theme explicit' and confounds the *libertins* by stating that the right sort of solitude 'can only exist in the absence of women, the agents of the most powerful voluptuous temptation'. But surely Eve is not Adam's mistress in either sense of the word: she is his wedded wife (Marvell says 'mate') and the poet does not here renounce love but marriage. We now know for certain, thanks to Professor F. S. Tupper, that the man Marvell stuck to the last by the wisdom then revealed to him. He remained so far a hedonist that he never married. As his eighteenth-century editor, Captain Thompson, R.N., put it for all time: 'He had no wife and his gallantries are not known.'

Questions

Pierre Legouis is the author of a critical biography, *Andrew Marvell, Poet, Puritan, Patroit*. This is a standard work, as will be Professor Legouis' forthcoming edition of Marvell (Oxford University Press), based on H. M. Margoliouth's texts. With Legouis' article, we are fully engaged in a critical battle over "The Garden." A basic problem with criticism on this the "most frequently re-examined of Marvell's poems" emerges in Legouis' discussion of William Empson's dyads. There are two meanings for everything, as Empson writes, and, as Mr. Legouis writes (p. 383), these might be labelled the "obvious" and the "improbable." The "obvious" is defined as "the historical meaning, the only one that Marvell meant, the obvious one for mid-seventeenth-century men." The "improbable" interpretation results from the tendencies of "New Critics" to apply non-historical and non-literary definitions as they read the poem.

> Where do you stand in this battle of critical methodologies? Do you think it is possible and/or desirable to read the poem as a mid-seventeenth century man would have read it?

> By comparing Legouis' criticism of Empson with his remarks on Kermode's essay, can you tell clearly what side he is on?

> Is Legouis' criticism directed, primarily, at the "errors" of particular writers, or at the arbitrariness of New Criticism in general?

Maren-Sofie Røstvig

Andrew Marvell's "The Garden": A Hermetic Poem*

Andrew Marvell's 'The Garden' has provoked more interpretative ingenuity on the part of contemporary scholars and critics than perhaps any other seventeenth-century lyric. The reasons are varied, but one contributive cause is surely to be found in the circumstance that so many of the now senescent 'new' critics have chosen to bury their teeth in it. Mr. Empson's discussion, in *Some Versions of Pastoral*, springs readily to mind, and among his followers interpretations have been spawned with a fertility little short of amazing. However, the literary historians have also enjoyed contributing their share, and of their work Miss Wallerstein's is perhaps the most monumental.[1]

The combatants are indeed numerous. Any publisher who might wish to print an anthology of critical exposition and commentary dealing with this one poem only, would be faced with a sufficiently formidable proposition. If it achieved nothing else, such a collection would at least provide interesting insights into early twentieth-century critical idioms and attitudes (not to say jargons), and might eventually lead to the adoption of a more chastened diction and a less exuberant fancy among the expositors of poems. It might also lead to a bridging of the gap between scholars and critics by exposing the weaknesses and the strengths of each.

---

*Parts of this essay first appeared in *English Studies*, XL (1959), 65-76, and in Professor Røstvig's *The Happy Man: Studies in the Metamorphoses of a Classical Ideal*. 2nd ed. New York: Humanities Press Inc., 1962, I, 161-72, and Oslo: Norwegian Universities Press, 1962. Professor Røstvig has revised and expanded "Andrew Marvell's 'The Garden': A Hermetic Poem" for this book. Students should use the title and page numbers from this casebook when citing or quoting the essay.

[1] *Studies in Seventeenth-Century Poetic* (University of Wisconsin Press, 1950).

Upon perusal of our imaginary anthology one interesting point would appear, to wit the fact that so many Marvell scholars have been puzzled by a contradiction between the stanzas that offer an austere, indeed almost ascetic vision of life, and those that seem to err in the direction of a voluptuous abandonment to the world of sense. It will be remembered that Marvell begins his poem with an impassioned apostrophe to the delicious solitude of the garden; next he denounces the stupid lovers who fail to see how far the beauties of the garden surpass those of a mortal woman, and finally he denounces erotic passion altogether in favour of a different kind of love ('When we have run our Passions heat, / Love hither makes his best retreat'). In the next stanza we expect a description of a non-erotic, elevated kind of love, but what do we get? This is surely no ascetic existence:

> What wond'rous Life in this I lead!
> Ripe Apples drop about my head;
> The Luscious Clusters of the Vine
> Upon my Mouth do crush their Wine;
> The Nectaren, and curious Peach,
> Into my hands themselves do reach;
> Stumbling on Melons, as I pass,
> Insnar'd with Flow'rs, I fall on Grass.

The 'garlands of repose,' it would seem, can be employed in the pursuit of sensual pleasure, and the amorous behaviour of the vegetable world more than compensates for the loss of a mere female mistress. To one critic, writing for *Scrutiny*, Marvell's garden, as described in this stanza, seemed 'a sort of giant fleshy orchid, deliciously hostile and unbridled by any rational end or discipline, which closes around the man and devours him'. A curious kind of sexual experience is hinted at when he adds that there is 'an ominous air of uncontrol about this picture of sensory pleasure, in which man becomes not agent but victim'.[2] And in a recent article in *ELH* Lawrence W. Hyman asks: 'What kind of garden is this where all the pleasures of passion can be enjoyed among trees and flowers, where plants are sexual and man is not? Despite the efforts of the critics, this central contradiction remains.'[3]

---

[2] Harold Wendell Smith, 'Cowley, Marvell, and the Second Temple,' *Scrutiny*, XIX (1953), 190. Smith's interpretation has been discussed by me in my article on 'Benlowes, Marvell, and the Divine Casimire,' *The Huntington Library Quarterly*, XVIII (1954), 13-35.

[3] L. W. Hyman, 'Marvell's *Garden*,' *ELH*, XXV (1958), 13. See also L. W. Hyman, *Andrew Marvell* (Twayne Publishers: New York, 1964), p. 68.

In an interesting attempt to solve this contradiction, L. W. Hyman applies the legend of the androgynous—or bi-sexual—Adam. This legend admittedly solves part of the puzzle. If one posits that Marvell was thinking of the time, before Eve was created, when Adam was supposed to have been bi-sexual, one understands why he describes this kind of solitude as 'delicious' and why he rejects the presence of Eve. 'When the poet enters the Garden, he is Adam in his innocent and androgynous state, walking about the Garden of Eden.'

In offering this solution Hyman does not claim originality, since Ruth Wallerstein had already referred to the same legend as a possible strand in the intellectual pattern of the poem. Much can be said in favour of Hyman's interpretation, which cannot be summarised here. My main objection is simply that his solution does not go far enough. More particularly, he fails to offer a sufficiently convincing explanation of the amorous behaviour of the vegetable world. He does not really succeed in explaining why plants make a better mistress than Eve. The circumstance that they reflect the androgynous state desired by the poet does not explain why *they* should pursue *him* so persistently with their love. This central problem still remains. It also remains to establish whether Marvell possibly was familiar with a specific literary source for the legend.

One possible source is the *Anatomy of Melancholy*, which refers to this particular piece of abstruse learning as to so many others. This work, however, presents only a passing reference. A much more likely source can be located in a work which so far has received but scant attention by scholars concerned with Marvell's poem. Yet once this source has been consulted it will be seen that the context in which the legend there is placed, offers a very satisfactory explanation of the amorous behaviour of the 'lovely green.' Moreover, in this source the androgynous state is given a spiritual explanation up to the ecstatic experience which forms the crux of the poem. Finally, it can actually be proved that Marvell must have been familiar with this particular work.

The source which I have in mind is one which is connected with Plato as well as with *Genesis* (works consulted by Hyman), in that it presents an account of the creation of the world in Platonic terms. It consists of a number of brief dialogues which the Renaissance believed to have been written, through divine revelation, by Hermes Trismegistus, a contemporary of Moses. We now know that the authors were pagan Platonists living as late as the third or fourth century after Christ, and that the pronounced similarity to many Biblical passages is due to a common basis in the philosophy of

Plato.[4] Ficino, who published the first Latin translation of the Greek
text in 1471, supposed that Plato had derived his theology from
Hermes through Pythagoras. The presence of a continuous demand
for the text is revealed by the fact that no less than twenty-two Latin
editions appeared between 1471 and 1641. And no wonder, since the
churchmen themselves recommended a close study of the Hermetic
corpus.

If we now turn to the Hermetic books, and particularly to the first
Libellus with its account of the creation of a totally androgynous
world, even a fairly cursory reading reveals that here we have mate-
rial which may serve to illuminate from within those intriguing
passages in 'The Garden' which have provoked so much interpreta-
tive cunning. As one reads on, one's conviction deepens that Marvell
must have been writing within a convention established by the
Hermetic, rather than the Mosaic, account of the Creation. However,
subjectively convincing as internal evidence may be, it will always
require objective corroboration to command general conviction. And,
interestingly enough, such corroborative external evidence is found if
one examines the conditions under which Marvell lived in the years
from 1651 to 1653—the period when he is generally supposed to have
written not only 'Upon the Hill and Grove at Bill-borow, To the Lord
Fairfax' and 'Upon Appleton House, to my Lord Fairfax', but also
'The Garden'. 'The Garden', too, is believed to be a poetic compli-
ment to Thomas, Lord Fairfax, in whose household Marvell spent
these years as a teacher of languages to the young Mary Fairfax.

Fairfax was a man with strong literary and religious interests; on
his retirement from active service in 1650 at the age of 38, he pro-
ceeded to put his leisure hours to account by composing metrical
versions of the Psalms and the Song of Solomon, and by translating
a French edition of, and commentary on, the Hermetic dialogues. On
entering the household of the Lord General, therefore, Marvell came
in direct contact with a milieu where religious piety found expres-
sion in the composition of religious verse and in the study of Her-
metic doctrines.

Since Renaissance Hermeticism may connect with the occult, as in
the case of Thomas Vaughan's alchemical writings, it must be under-
lined that by far the strongest impulse was to believe that the doc-
trines expressed by Hermes were in agreement with those of the

---

[4] See the introduction to Walter Scott, ed., *Hermetica* (Oxford, 1924-36). The
dialogues may contain material dating back to a much earlier period according to
S. G. F. Brandon, "The Gnostic Problem in Early Christianity," *History Today*, X
(June, 1960), 415-23.

Church. This belief fired all Renaissance editors and commentators, beginning with Ficino (1471) and Lefèvre d'Etaples (1494 and 1505), whose comments on the perfectly orthodox character of Hermetic doctrines were echoed with the greatest fidelity by subsequent editors. This is true of the Italian edition by Tommaso Benci (1548), and of the French translation by Gabriel du Preau (1549). The collection of dialogues entitled the *Pimander* was published in its original Greek text by Turnèbe in 1554, and in 1574 a second edition appeared, edited by François de Foix with the aid of Scaliger. (This edition contained a French translation and a new translation into Latin as well.) François de Foix, Bishop of Aire and Duke of Candale, is a key figure in the history of Renaissance Hermeticism; the commentary which he published at Bourdeaux in 1579 (*Le Pimandre de Mercure de la Philosophie Chrestienne*), although both long and learned, is much more pleasant to read than the three-volume commentary by Hannibal Rosselus published at Cracow in 1585-1586 (*Pymander Mercurii Trismegisti Cum Commento*). The work which fascinated Fairfax to such an extent that he attempted a translation, is the commentary by François de Foix, and it is reasonable to assume that his interest must have been stirred by Dr. John Everard's translation of the *Pimander* into English in 1650. Proof of Fairfax's familiarity with this translation is afforded by the fact that Fairfax made use of it in his own translation. Instead of grappling with the problem of translating the Hermetic text as rendered in French by de Foix, he simply copied out the English version already published by Everard. Since every paragraph in this text is accompanied by many pages of learned commentary, one understands that Fairfax might well want to concentrate on the commentary rather than the text. Everard's translation had made the text accessible; what was needed, was a reliable commentary. The purpose of this commentary is made explicit in the preface, where de Foix out-Ficinos Ficino in the claims he advances concerning the orthodox character of the dialogues and the genuinely divine inspiration which they contain. Their account of creation is in complete agreement with Genesis, and so is their presentation of the Fall and the scheme of redemption by the son of God. Hermes taught doctrines agreeable to God, and he even obtained salvation by the same means as a true Christian.[5]

---

[5] The unknown author of the preface to Everard's translation, J. F., maintains that "In this Book . . . is contained more true knowledg of God and Nature, then in all the Books in the World besides, I except onely Sacred Writ." *The Divine Pymander Of Hermes Trismegistus . . . Translated . . . By that Learned Divine Doctor Everard* (London, 1650), sig. [A₅v].

That this belief in the validity of the "revelation" contained in the Hermetic dialogues prevailed also outside the narrow circle of learned commentators, can be seen on turning for example to Sir Walter Raleigh's *A History of the World* (1614), or again to David Person's *Varieties* (1635). Although Casaubon's *Exercitationes* (London, 1614) exploded the myth of the extreme antiquity of these written records, his general argument nevertheless very much strengthened the popular belief that they contain Christian truths.

Since Fairfax undertook the labour of trying to convey, in English, what de Foix had written in French, we must needs believe that he shared this attitude, like so many of his contemporaries. As a professional linguist and man of letters Marvell could easily have been involved in almost daily discussions of various aspects of the Hermetic dialogues as interpreted by the French nobleman and prelate. Such a situation would certainly explain why Marvell, in his poetic compliments to Fairfax, included so many allusions to concepts of vital importance in the Hermetic tradition. Nor was literary precedent for so doing absent. Marvell may have been ignorant of the fact that a poet like Henry Vaughan was incorporating Hermetic material into his verse, but he was clearly familiar with the works of the most celebrated neo-Latin poet of his age, Casimire Sarbiewski, in whose Horatian odes and epodes Hermetic ideas are encountered.[6] Marvell, therefore, could have been inspired by this literary example of a successful fusion between classical themes and forms and Christian sentiments of a Platonic or Hermetic cast.

After these preliminary remarks let us turn to the test of internal evidence. Is it actually possible to submit a largely Hermetic interpretation of Marvell's poem, and, if so, will such an interpretation succeed in discovering unity and coherence where so far we have tended to see a paradoxical juxtaposition of irreconcilable attitudes?

My analysis will take as its point of departure the strong contrast drawn in the first two stanzas between the 'uncessant Labours' of men in society on the one hand, and, on the other, 'delicious Solitude', 'Fair quiet', and the 'Garlands of repose'. This contrast between a meditative, introvert existence and a worldly, busy life is of course frequently enough encountered in impeccably Christian contexts, and no doubt the strong insistence in the Hermetic dialogues on a complete withdrawal from the world and from physical existence

---

[6] See the article by me referred to in footnote 2, and also Chapters III and IV of Vol. I of my study of *The Happy Man* (2nd revised ed. 1962). For translations of Casimire's odes, see Vaughan, *Olar Iscanus* (1651) and G. Hills, *The Odes of Casimire* (1646) as reproduced in Number 44 of the publications of the Augustan Reprint Society (Los Angeles, 1953).

was felt as proof of their agreement with Holy Writ.[7] These dialogues present the establishment of complete silence and bodily repose as the first step towards regeneration, and regeneration in its turn is seen as a re-establishment of the reign of mind over matter, or (to use Biblical terminology) of spiritual man over carnal man. When this has been achieved, union with the Deity may follow. The vision of the Deity, so one reads in Everard's translation of 1650, induces "a Divine Silence, and the rest of all the Senses: For neither can he that understands that, understand anything else, nor he that see that, see any thing else, nor hear any other thing, nor in sum, move the Body."[8] The first Hermetic *libellus* begins with the description of such an ecstatic experience, in the course of which the body no longer functions but is as it were completely paralysed. The commentary by de Foix compares this experience to that of the prophet Daniel and again to that of St. Paul on his way to Damascus, where (as Fairfax puts it) "by a vision he was cast to the ground, deprived of all strength & corporal facultys, nothing remaining in him but the use of reason, understanding, & other intellectual powers."[9] Silence is important, since by its means the 'intelligible powers' peculiar to man "are maintained in their vigour, & garded from all hindrences and perturbation of speech." These powers are diverted from their proper function by "extravagant words unprofitable, or vitious." Before sin was introduced, God "was knowne, praysed, and reverenced" by silence.[10]

The concepts that we are discussing—'Fair quiet', 'repose', and 'delicious Solitude'—should also be related to the Hermetic view of the dual nature of man. Since man is compounded both of matter and mind, he is mortal and immortal at the same time. It is the mortal part that insists on the pursuit of inferior pleasures ('the Palm, the Oke, or Bayes'); the immortal part reveals itself only 'While all Flow'rs and all Trees do close / To weave the Garlands of repose.'

To understand the curious relationship between the poet and 'this lovely green' (stanzas 3, 4, and 5), it is necessary to give a brief summary of the Hermetic account of the creation of man.

---

[7] François de Foix presumes that the dialogues were written before the Holy Scriptures, which makes their agreement a remarkable fact. See Mercurius Trismegistus Pimander, translated by Thomas Lord Fairfax, British Museum MS Number 25447, page [3^v].

[8] Everard, *op. cit.*, p. 44 (From IV, 17).

[9] Fairfax, *op. cit.*, from the comments on the opening lines. Two marginal glosses read: "The extasie of Mercury discrib'd" and "Revelation made to Mercury in an extasie." Marginal references to corresponding Biblical passages underline the thesis concerning the agreement between the Hermetic dialogues and Holy Writ.

[10] Fairfax, p. [64^v].

During the first stage in his development man was mind only, like God. However, soon after his creation man penetrated downwards through the seven planetary spheres until he reached the earth. There he sees reflected 'the fair and beautiful Shape or Form of God' and falls in love with it. This reflection is that of his own mind, which is immortal and divine and part of God. On seeing 'a shape like unto himself' reflected in the watery element, man 'loved it, and would cohabit with it; and immediately upon the resolution, ensued the Operation.'[11] As a result of this union was created man's 'unreasonable Image or Shape', that is an image devoid of reason because composed of matter only. The interesting fact at this point is this: not only is man in love with Nature, because it reflects the image of God and hence also of his own mind, but Nature itself loves man when it sees the reflection of God in him: 'Nature presently laying hold of what it so much loved, did wholly wrap her self about it, and they were mingled, for they loved one another.'[12] One now sees exactly why 'No white nor red was ever seen / So am'rous as this lovely green', and why the poet submits to its passionate embrace. As in the Hermetic account, the sexual embrace reflects a union between the images of God in man and in Nature.

It is at this stage in the history of the creation of man that it is explicitly stated that man is an androgyne. In the words of Fairfax, 'being male & female, in the same body as the Scriptures said of the first man before he siñed & before god took the woman out of the side of man.'[13] All creatures, moreover, shared this bi-sexual structure and retained it for a certain unspecified period. During this period they were tied in a certain bond or knot which, in the words of Fairfax, 'held all things from action, poyse or motion'.[14] Since this bi-sexual stage prevents all beings from indulging in action (forces them to enjoy the garlands of repose, as it were), it possesses a profound spiritual significance. While it is the property of matter to move, the mind is utterly quiescent. The androgynous state, therefore, is one in which matter is subordinated to mind. When Marvell in his poem explicitly rejects motion, or physical pursuit (whether of honour or of women), in favour first of repose and then of a state 'without a Mate', we can be sure that Fairfax would have grasped the Hermetic context immediately. He would at once have seen that the Earthly Paradise visualised by Marvell reflects the androgynous period during

---

11 Everard, *op. cit.*, p. 21. From Book II, paragraphs 23-24.
12 *Ibid.*, p. 21. Book II, par. 25.
13 Fairfax, p. [42ᵛ].
14 *Ibid.*, p. [44ᵛ].

which the divine element in the Creation reigned supreme, and when this element was mutually recognised and loved on all levels, whether animate or inanimate.

The androgynous period, however, was destined to come to an end, and so 'the bond of all things was loosed and untied by the Will of God . . . and so the Males were apart by themselves, and the Females likewise.'[15] Subsequently God commands all creatures to increase and to multiply (i.e. to engage in action or motion), but with this important caution attached: '. . . let him that is endued with Minde, know himself to be immortal; and that the cause of death is the love of the body.'[16]

If one returns to Marvell's poem with these passages in mind, one sees how pregnant with meaning his lines are. The usual type of mortal lover is 'fond' or stupid because he permits his soul to be engrossed by the vastly inferior love of the body, which is the cause of death. He is ignorant and cruel because he does not know himself or the true character of the Creation. He sees neither his own divinity nor that of the trees. Only the man who sharpens his intellectual powers through silence and bodily repose sees how far the beauty of 'this lovely green' exceeds that of women. Man, to him, is revealed as a 'mortal God'[17] just as nature becomes a 'material God'.[18] The amorous green, moreover, does not tempt him to lose his true identity as a mortal God by succumbing to the world of sense. Man's erotic or sexual passion, he realises, is nothing but a thoroughly undesirable preoccupation with the world of sense and motion. Indeed, the act of generation is in itself evil: 'For all things that are made or generated, are full of Passion; . . . and where Passion is there is not the Good; where the Good is, there is no Passion.'[19] Hence Marvell writes with admirable Hermetic logic: 'When we have run our Passions heat, / Love hither makes his best retreat.' The true good, in other words, is in the garden, in silence, physical repose, and in loving communion with the 'sacred green'.[20] The purpose of Marvell's re-enactment, in stanza 5, of that first passionate embrace between

---

[15] Everard, *op. cit.*, p. 23 f. From II, 37.

[16] *Ibid.*, p. 24. From II, 38.

[17] *Ibid.*, p. 60. From IV, 93.

[18] *Ibid.*, p. 48. From IV, 37.

[19] *Ibid.*, p. 74. From VI, 10.

[20] The phrase is Casimire's. For a description of the 'sacred green' which woos man, see Casimire's Ode IV, 21 (a paraphrase of a passage taken from '*Salomon's* sacred marriage song') as translated by G. Hills in his *Odes of Casimire* (London, 1646), pp. 83-89. Here, as elsewhere, Casimire's descriptions of Nature are pervaded by Hermetic concepts. His amorous green woos not only man, but also the wandering stars and the sun (cp. his first epode).

mind and matter seems to be to receive a taste of that purer love or
communion which can be experienced only when the passions of the
body have been stilled. This communion is apparently possible
between superior and inferior parts of the Creation. 'But there is a
communion of Souls', so Hermes says, 'and those of God, communicate
with those [of] men; and those of men, with those of Beasts . . .
Therefore is the World subject unto God, Man unto the World, and
unreasonable things to Man.'[21] And after having received mental
illumination Tat, the son of Hermes, discovers that he is one with
the entire Creation: 'I am in living Creatures, in Plants, in the Womb,
every where.'[22]

The process of purification or illumination through silence, repose,
and communion with the amorous green leads logically to the
climactic experience when the mind succeeds in 'Casting the Bodies
Vest aside'. Marvell's description in this part of his poem, too,
becomes much clearer if one relates it to the Hermetic exposition of
the relationship between the mind and the body.

The Hermetic philosophy distinguishes between mind, soul, spirit,
and body—the soul and the spirit forming intermediate stages between
pure mind and pure matter. The mind informs the soul, and the soul
is connected with the body through the spirit, which in its turn is
diffused and passes through the veins and the arteries of the body.[23]
The mind, it must be remembered, 'is of the very Essence of God' and
hence 'is not cut off, or divided from the essentiality of God, but
united as the light of the Sun.'[24] The mind therefore forms an ocean
where 'each kind / Does streight its own resemblance find', just as the
mind in its turn once had viewed its own image in the waters of
the earth and thus had been led to cohabit with gross matter. 'Its
own resemblance' would seem to be the image of God, since this
image is in all things even in the inanimate world. The belief that the
entire Creation is penetrated by soul is perhaps the most distinctive
aspect of the Hermetic philosophy:

---

21 Everard, *op. cit.*, p. 57 f. From IV, 77 and 79.
22 *Ibid.*, p. 89. From VII, 47.
23 'The Mind, which is immortal, cannot establish or rest it self, naked, and of it
self, in an Earthly Body; neither is the Earthly Body able to bear such immortality:
And therefore, that it might suffer so great vertue, the Minde compacted as it
were, and took to it self the passible Body of the Soul, as a Covering or a Cloath-
ing. And the Soul being also in some sort Divine, useth the Spirit as her Minister
and Servant: and the Spirit governeth the living thing.' *Ibid.*, p. 53 f. From IV, 59.
24 *Ibid.*, p. 138 f. From XI, 1 and 3.

> All this Universal Body, in which are all Bodies is full of Soul,
>   the Soul full of Minde, the Minde full of God.
> For within he fills them, and without he contains them,
>   quickening the Universe . . .
> For there is nothing which is not the Image of God . . .
> For therefore hath he made all things, that thou by all things
>   mayest see him.
> This is the Good of God, this is his Vertue, to appear,
>   and to be seen in all things.[25]

To summarise: In his mind man is united with God and with all
creatures, animate or inanimate, and these creatures in their turn see
the reflection of their own souls in the general ocean formed by the
principle of mind. And once the proper degree of bodily repose has
been achieved, it is possible for the mind to 'Withdraw into its
happiness', that is, to withdraw into that part of the Creation which
is God by dismissing 'the Bodies Vest'. In this moment the communion
experienced in stanza five becomes absolute and complete. It becomes
a complete union not only with God, but also with all the creatures
and with the creative principle itself. This creative principle was not
exhausted with the creation of man and the world, hence it comprises
also 'Far other Worlds, and other Seas'. Through the process of
withdrawal, 'all that's made' is annihilated to 'a green Thought in a
green Shade'. This may possibly again be a reference to the rejection
of that mortal aspect of the world which stands reflected in the
division between males and females, and to the divine quality of
bi-sexuality, a quality which very well may be referred to as 'green'
since the vegetable world is the only part of creation which has
retained its bi-sexual structure. And this bi-sexual structure in its
turn represents the creative principle. This is underlined by de Foix
in his commentary on *Libellus I*, section 12, where he refers to God,
adding: '(which was sayd before to have in him selfe both sexes)
that is to say all power of production without any succour, or
exteriour ayde.'[26] By thus associating bi-sexuality with the creative
principle, the legend of the androgynous Adam is again made the
vehicle of profound spiritual insight.

But to return to the garden ecstasy. One notices that it is the soul
which glides into the boughs; the mind is not released in its naked

---

25 *Ibid.*, p. 136 f.
26 Fairfax, p. (23r).

and divine state, it is still dressed in the soul as in a 'Covering or a Cloathing'.[27] The mind can be completely released only by the death of the body. The ecstasy which is experienced while in the body, yet out of it, consists in a release of the *soul*. Interestingly enough, the mind after death puts on a *fiery coat*, fire being its proper element. Pure mind 'hath the fire for its Body'.[28] In this circumstance one may possibly find an explanation of the 'various Light' which Marvell's soul 'Waves in its Plumes'. The fiery body of the mind shines through the outer garment of the soul, waiting for death, or 'longer flight', before it can be released.[29]

It is significant that Marvell directly associates 'that happy Garden-state' with the ecstatic movement by adding a stanza on the Garden of Eden after the ecstasy has been completed. The implication is clearly that both the garden-state and the ecstasy consist in the reign of mind over matter. That the ecstasy consists in the release of the soul is a religious commonplace, but that the Earthly Paradise should symbolise a similar state is an idea closely associated only with Hermetic doctrines. When one adds the concept of the androgynous character of the Creation to this idea—as Marvell himself does in stanza 8—the identification becomes complete. As far as I know, this particular juxtaposition of ideas can be found in no other context. The rejection of Eve, then, is no mere rejection of female companionship in favour of masculine solitude. It is a rejection of the reign of matter, symbolised by the act of generation, and an acceptance, instead, of that bi-sexual structure which man and the rest of the creatures originally shared with God, but which God alone retained together with the vegetable world.[30] As soon as man became mortal he could no longer remain solitary, since his mortality was the result of the division into two sexes. Hence ' 'twas beyond a Mortal's share / To wander solitary there.'

---

27 See footnote 23.

28 Everard, *op. cit.*, p. 54. From IV, 60—62.

29 In the moment of death 'the Spirit is contracted into the blood, and the Soul into the Spirit; but the Minde being pure, and free from these cloathings; and being Divine by Nature, taking a fiery Body, rangeth abroad in every place, leaving the Soul to judgment, and to the punishment it hath deserved.' *Ibid.*, p. 52. From IV, 56. It must be explained that the soul deserves punishment if it has permitted itself to love the body and hence to become corrupt.

30 It is in keeping with the peculiar quality of Marvell's wit to interpret the concluding couplet of stanza 8 ('Two Paradises 'twere in one / To live in Paradise alone') as a clever allusion to bi-sexuality. For examples of the use of Paradise as a metaphor for the sexual organs, see John Ford, *'Tis Pity She's a Whore* (Regents Renaissance Drama Series, 1966), II, i, lines 42-49 and Pope, *Epistle to Burlington*, lines 145-148.

When thus related to that Hermetic philosophy which Fairfax laboured to elucidate, Marvell's lines fall into a coherent and fascinating pattern. His rejection of women and of the passions of the body has now been placed in a context which explains why it is possible to turn from a rejection of sex and the world of sense in one moment, to a frankly erotic intercourse with the 'lovely green' in the next. This 'central contradiction' now has completely vanished. It is important to realise that Hermetic ideas do not occur here and there in isolated lines; they carry the entire poem. For a man like Fairfax (and, one imagines, Henry Vaughan) it would have been mere child's play to catch the various allusions. He would at once have seen that the ulterior purpose of Marvell's retirement was to effect a process of regeneration whereby the mind is released from its subjection to the body.

The final emblematic picture of the garden with its fragrant zodiac drives home the point of the entire poem with concrete forcefulness. In these lines Marvell may be glancing at Claudian's well-known and popular epigram on the old man from Verona: 'Happy the Man, who his whole time doth bound / Within th'enclosure of his little ground.'[31] This man refuses to embark on foolish wanderings, and is content to observe the passing of the seasons and the time of day in the surrounding landscape rather than by means of calendars or dials: 'He measures time by Landmarks, and has found / For the whole day the Dial of his ground.' Benlowes, too, had made this point.[32] However, in Marvell's poem the sundial and the fragrant zodiac are made to convey a profound religious lesson. Thus the 'skilful Gardner' and his plot of ground become a type of God and the Creation, the visible sun a symbol of the invisible Deity. Just as man's physical eye looks to the sun and stars to compute the time, his mind looks to the Divine Mind to trace the progress of the invisible angelic world. In this manner the visible shadows forth the invisible. The world of bees and flowers is equally governed by the sun; in other words, even the lower level of intelligence assigned to the animal and vegetable worlds is capable of communion with the stars. The importance of rightly computing time by studying the heavenly bodies is stressed by Plato, who maintains that the result of this process will be to reproduce the same ordered motion in the mind of him who computes. The 'milder Sun' is a pregnant phrase. The disciples of Plato and Hermes looked upon the visible

---

[31] The translation is Abraham Cowley's.
[32] *Theophila* (1652), XII, 96.

sun as the shadow of God,[33] as God's physical counterpart in the realm of matter. During his ecstasy, the poet has for a while contemplated the Sun of the sun and been one with it, sharing its creative power. Hence his attitude of benign approval in the concluding stanza, so reminiscent of the attitude of God on the seventh day of creation, and hence also his allusion to the physical sun as necessarily 'milder'.

So far, I have almost completely overlooked the more orthodox religious ideas, although the similarity between stanza 5 and the traditional paraphrases of *Canticles* is obvious. For this reason the traditional theological interpretation of *Canticles* must be taken into account. Marvell's ripe apples recall the Earthly Paradise described by Casimire and Benlowes, whose apples were free from the taste of death by virtue of the fruit of the tree of the cross, that fruit which set at nought the effect of the fatal apple eaten by Adam and Eve. The luscious clusters of the vine may be interpreted as a reference to Christ, while the embrace between the poet and the *res creatae* shadows forth the mystic marriage between the soul and Christ. The fruit tree at whose foot the poet is placed, would in this case be the tree of the Cross (Christ being its 'fruit'), the fountain the baptismal waters or the waters of redemption and regeneration. If this traditional symbolism is seen as valid for Marvell's poem, then Marvell would seem to be contemplating the deepest mystery of the Christian faith—the mystery of Christ on the cross, the moment of that supreme sacrifice when the Saviour divested Himself of the "Bodies Vest." When the contemplated object and the contemplating mind become one,[34] the poet's mind ascends the tree, where "like a Bird it sits, and sings."

It would be anachronistic to assume that these orthodox religious ideas conflict with those that are Hermetic; with François de Foix and Thomas, Lord Fairfax we must necessarily assume that they are in perfect agreement. One may dismiss the Hermetic interpretation presented here, but *not* for the reason that it represents an occult tradition, as Frank Kermode has argued,[35] the conflict between

---

[33] This is a commonplace also in orthodox theology, where Christ is presented as the *sol iustitiæ* according to *Malachi* 4:2. A Hermetic philosopher like Robert Fludd (*Philosophia Moysaica*, 1638) returns again and again to *Psalm* 19:4-6, a passage interpreted as Biblical proof of the correctness of the association between Christ and the sun. A good example of the Platonic view that God is the Sun of the sun is found in Ficino, *Opera Omnia* (Paris, 1641), I, 596 ("Sol Solis est Deus. . .").

[34] Plotinus, *The Enneads*, III, viii, 8.

[35] Frank Kermode, "Introduction," *The Selected Poetry of Marvell* (Signet Classics: New York, 1967), p. xx.

mind and body being taken to represent a dualism unacceptable to Christian thought. Whoever turns to the commentary written by François de Foix will discover that statements conveying a gnostic dualism are glossed so as to agree with the teaching of Christ. Thus de Foix identifies the Hermetic praise of the world of pure mind with Paul's concept of the "inward man" obedient to the law of God (*Rom.* 7:22), just as he interprets the Hermetic denunciation of the body as a reference to that symbolic crucifixion of carnal man whereby the new man is born. The contrast between carnal and spiritual man—a theme which informs the impassioned sermons of Dr. John Everard—was a primary concern of Marvell's generation, and it is scarcely surprising that he should have accepted the mind-body conflict as a profoundly Christian theme. That the shutting of the eyes brings true light exceeding the splendour of the sun is an idea strongly stressed in the Hermetic dialogues, but it is also frequently found in religious treatises with a mystical bias. We find exactly the same fusion of Christian with Hermetic and/or Platonic concepts in the imagery of a poem like Henry Vaughan's "The World," for the simple reason that Vaughan, too, shared the syncretistic belief in the agreement between these philosophical traditions and Christian thought. Renaissance syncretism, as it extends from Cusanus and Ficino in the fifteenth century to Dr. John Everard and Henry More in the seventeenth, possessed a strong poetic appeal. This appeal is felt the moment that one reads a commented Renaissance edition of the *Pimander*, a work which concludes with a *chant de nombre octonaire* in praise of God, the structural number eight being in imitation of the structure of Psalm 119 as de Foix explains. Before Tat is permitted to listen to this hymn, he must seek absolute bodily repose and he must also close all his senses to the world, thus "annihilating all that's made." He must retire into the secret places of the mind, contemplating that which cannot be perceived by the senses. Whoever plunges into the basin of the divine mind is made a partaker of the divine wisdom, by means of which he contemplates God. According to de Foix what happens is that the Holy Ghost enters into the contemplating soul, deifying it, which cannot take place "sans auoir auparauant despouillé la chair, corps & matiere." All movement, action, and passion must be abandoned. Augustine presented a similar argument in his *De vera religione*, xxxv, 65 as was only to be expected from a man who approved of Hermes as well as Plato—an approval frequently cited by Renaissance writers with a syncretistic bias.

This article was prompted by the desire to find a source, if possible, for Marvell's use of the legend of the androgynous Adam. As a result of this quest it now seems apparent that Marvell drew upon a Christianised version of Hermetic doctrines for key concepts or images. Until a thorough study has been made of Renaissance syncretism it will be difficult to assess the extent to which these concepts must be regarded as mere commonplaces rather than as esoteric lore accessible only to the few. My own research has led me to favour the first alternative rather than the second, and if this view is accepted, two consequences follow: (1) a poem labelled as "Hermetic" must nevertheless be considered as within the reach of a fairly large number of readers, and (2) such a poem must not be classified as occult and interpreted in the light of what we now know about the true character of Hermetic doctrines. These doctrines must be studied through the commentaries available *at the time,* and in the case of Marvell the logical point of departure is the fact that Fairfax not only possessed a copy of one such commentary, but that he actually translated part of it into English.

Marvell's outstanding ability as a poet is revealed by the fact that our twentieth-century ignorance of Renaissance syncretism is no bar to our enjoyment of his verse. The well-known theme of the happiness of retirement is easily recognised, and so is the superior quality of the treatment that Marvell gives to it. On this vital point there can be no disagreement.

Questions

Maren-Sofie Røstvig writes from Norway, north of the critics' battleground, yet she is clearly aware of the critical conventions, or norms, which have risen to surround "The Garden." The camps are divided into literary historians, students of the *genre*, the historians of ideas, and the New Critics. In this essay, Professor Røstvig's scholarship is primarily in the field of intellectual history. Her findings are linked to "The Garden" by both an intrinsic study of the poem and the support of historical evidence. As if in response to Pierre Legouis' request, Røstvig's essay sets out to establish a mid-seventeenth century context for Marvell's poem. By describing the scholarly interests of General Fairfax, the effort is made to provide us with a language and set of meanings which could have been of interest to Marvell when he wrote "The Garden." The essay then approaches the poem through doctrines and ideology of the legendary Hermes Trismegistus. We are grateful to Professor Røstvig for this revised and expanded text.

> If Thomas Fairfax can be considered as the ideal model for a mid-seventeenth-century reader, are you convinced that he would have read Andrew Marvell's "The Garden" as "A Hermetic Poem"?

What parallels can you draw between renaissance Hermeticism and the Christian and Neo-Platonic texts cited by Ruth Wallerstein and Milton Klonsky? Judging from his criticism of Klonsky, how would Pierre Legouis be likely to respond to your set of parallels?

Does your reading of "The Garden" establish that Marvell was concerned with the bi-sexual nature of the original, Eve-less Adam?

The continuity of critical views on this poem depends, generally, on one writer's respect for another's findings as well as a willingness not to reject his predecessor's method of analysis. Disagreement in literary criticism usually centers on one of these two grounds. If it is the latter, distinct "schools" of critics develop, each believing in its own distinct *way* of proving or establishing the probability of interpretations. By now you should be able to define, roughly:

1. literary history and genre study
2. history of ideas in literature
3. intrinsic analysis and the New Criticism.

Stanley N. Stewart

Marvell and
"The Garden Enclosed"*

In the preceding chapters we have explored a range of associated meanings potentially conveyed by a particular image-cluster in a particular Jacobean linguistic context. Though I believe the reticulations of such a context to be interesting as objects of our inquiry in their own right, the purpose of this book has been to show how an awareness of the complex associations of a context enriches (and, by implication, necessarily alters) our conception of a work of art, once that work of art has properly been placed within that context. The examples in this book—drawn from what is in effect a sublanguage of English, with its own lexicon, and its own rules for the use of each word—confront us with potentially relevant analogies, whose relevance may only be decided when we engage a particular poem and ask a particular question about its meaning.

I do not mean to say that the relevance of this context necessarily predicates our belief that the author of a poem intended to invoke the full range of possible associated meanings. To be sure, not every garden in seventeenth-century literature conjured fantasies of Solomon's enclosed pleasance, with its luscious, delightful, soul-saving shade; Campion's "There is a garden in her face" is an interesting poem, but the imagery here functions in its own way—one different, I think, from that discussed in this book: if "allegory" is to be a useful term, we must be able to distinguish /153/ metaphoric language which is not allegorical.[1] On the other hand, wherever a text is properly construed—even in part—in the context of the Song of

---

*Reprinted from *The Enclosed Garden* (Madison: The University of Wisconsin Press; © 1966 by the Regents of the University of Wisconsin), pp. 152-171, 176-181. Reprinted by permission of the publisher and the author.

Songs, then an aspect of the meaning of that text (and therefore part of its complexity) will be allegorical. This is an important point when we consider by all means the most complex, most subtle lyric written within the tradition of hortus conclusus, Andrew Marvell's "The Garden." For in this incredibly delicate and complex poem a number of relevant contexts converge, and Marvell holds them all in poised balance, echoing the *libertin* pastoral here, parodying it there, alluding to the occult in one moment, turning to the Christian in the next. The poem is shaped as a meditation (and in this way it is wholly different from the several Christian pastorals of Thomas Randolph), and throughout its imagery tantalizingly suggests the lush, garden eroticism of the allegorized Song of Songs.

Marvell's poem has mystified critics, who have in recent years approached the text with an enormous range of methods, running from impressionism (the garden is like a giant fleshly orchid, ready to devour man) to suggestions that "The Garden" ought to be compared with "Ode on a Grecian Urn."[2] It has been described as light and ominous in tone, as disjunct and unified in structure, as Plotinian, Hermetic, Buddhist, libertin and antilibertin in thought. Whether or not we take this range of testimony as an indication of the poem's complexity, or as a sign of the limits of human knowledge, one fact of importance to criticism remains: as each critic approaches the text he asserts, whether implicitly or explicitly, the relevance of a particular context to the act of construing the text. And as the context changes (Plotinus, Randolph, Montaigne, Freud), so does the "meaning" of the text. Of course, we need not argue that critical accord will descend once critics discover the poem's "true" or "total meaning,"[3] as if that essence has hovered for centuries in the pure realm of air, awaiting the incantation of a proper sensibility to summon it into substantial being. But it is proper to suppose that critics have not always recognized the relevant context of "The Garden," not always fully understood the implications of that context once its relevance has been established.

For example, one aspect of the poem has almost wholly been /154/ ignored: its allegorical meaning. Yet Ruth Wallerstein once stated that "the literature of the *hortus conclusus* . . . contributes the most" to the immediate context of "The Garden."[4] At the same time (as if in answer to William Empson), she insisted that the poem must not be taken as "an allegory of the Fall of Man," for it is, instead, "a lyric study of Marvell's experience." In this chapter I will try to show not only that the context of the Song of Songs is relevant to a proper understanding of "The Garden" but that,

because it is, the allegorical dimension of the poem's meaning ought
not to be ignored. For the context of the Song of Songs, as Marvell
received and used it, was, above all other things, distinctly allegorical.

Much of the critical argument over the poem concerns the passivity
of Marvell's speaker, especially as depicted in Stanza V. Radically
divided in their explanations of that passivity, the critics see it
variously as an expression of Marvell's sexual ambivalence, a refer-
ence to the Fall of man, an allusion to the idea of the hermaphro-
ditism of nature. Thus, one critic points to Freud, another to
Bonaventure, another to Randolph, still another to Hermes, and so
on. But despite this variety, most critics agree on the underlying
importance of a single question: In what sense is this "mystical"
poem to be construed as sexual? The attractiveness of the Hermetic
hypothesis arises from its relevance to this question; but in spite of
the now numerous ventures into Hermetic—and, for that matter,
Plotinian—writings, the question remains as vexed as before. For
even if the speaker is androgynous (indeed, especially if he is),
why should the garden pursue him rather than vice versa? Would
not androgyny imply an equal balance of give-and-take in love?
If so, we are left with the question of why the speaker is (as
he most certainly is) the passive recipient of the garden's affection.
The question might more properly be put in this way: What is the
relation between the speaker's passivity and the imagery which
conveys that passivity? And here the context of the Song of Songs
sheds light on Marvell's text.

We know that Marvell was familiar with this tradition; echoes
from Solomn's Song are heard in "The Nymph Complaining,"[5] and,
as Don Cameron Allen has shown, in "Appleton House" Marvell
uses the figure of hortus conclusus to intensify his satiric /155/ attack
on convent life. Thus, as in the Middle Ages, nunnery, cloister, and
virginity still represent separation from the world, but now Marvell
caustically alters the convention, suggesting that the completely
separated life leads to sterility. Professor Allen shows how the
theme of sterilty refers also to Fairfax, whose withdrawal from
public life gave Marvell pause, and perhaps led him to a serious
consideration of the values of the contemplative life.[6] At about the
same time—as Marvell was writing "The Garden" and serving as
tutor to Mary Fairfax—Lord Fairfax (who turned his hand also to
paraphrasing Proverbs) was rendering the Song of Songs into verse.

Fairfax's "Songe of Salomon" appears, along with numerous re-
ligious lyrics ("The Songe of Mary The Blessed Virgin," for instance)
in Bodleian MS. Fairfax 40. The paraphrase, itself neither better

nor worse than most, emphasizes the erotic qualities of Solomon's Song: "Kiss me ô kiss me with thy mouth," "I am my spouse into my Garden Come," "I held him fast & would not let him goe." Miss Røstvig suggests the likelihood not only that Marvell read his patron's poetic efforts but that the two men shared their views on the esoteric subjects presently concerning each of them (at the time, Fairfax was also quite involved with the *Hermetica*).[7] Such an exchange of ideas would, of course, place an interest in the Song of Songs quite close to Marvell's thinking at the time he was writing "The Garden." For in Fairfax's "Songe of Salomon," we have a typical verse paraphrase describing the lusciousness of the tree which offers its fruit and shade to the Beloved, who passively enjoys her "delightful seat." Again, in the allegorical context in which Fairfax was working, the qualities of the garden referred to aspects of the matchless Bride:

> My Love is as a Garding Loocked up
> Or springing fountaine that is sealed up
> Whose plants as orchards of pomgranets are
> With other fruits that pretious are and rare
> Cipresse & Spinknard wholsome safferron
> Calamus & Frankincense sweet cinamon
> Mirrh Aloes what else is of greatest price
> With numerous kinds of other cheifest spice
> A fount of Gardins Living springs that streme.[8]

/156/ More persuasive evidence that "The Garden" should be understood in this context is found in comparison between "The Garden" and Marvell's earlier Latin poem, "Hortus." Although for centuries "The Garden" was believed to be an English translation of the Latin poem, not since A. H. King's article in *English Studies* in 1938 has close study been made of the relation between these poems. It is generally agreed that "Hortus" was written about a year before "The Garden." Margoliouth has pointed to the inconvenience of the theory (held by Grosart among others)[9] that "The Garden" is a translation of "Hortus"; despite their marked similarities, the poems differ in both structure and imagery. Again, long sections present in Latin do not appear in the English poem; and the latter contains four stanzas for which no Latin counterparts exist. Serious consideration of these differences can lead to but one conclusion: as Marvell "translated" his poem he also revised it, and in so doing he created an entirely new artifact, a poem not only more Christian in content but bearing a markedly mediative tone and structure. Finally, Marvell's revision introduced an entirely new linguistic context in which the English poem must be read if it is to be properly understood.

Since this is a crucial point in my argument, it may be profitable to consider these revisions in some detail. "Hortus" is in most respects a classical poem of retirement. Not so "The Garden." Many of the most traditional sections of the Latin poem were eliminated by Marvell's revision. This passage, for example:

> *Me quoque, vos* Musae, &, *te conscie testor* Apollo,
> *Non Armenta juvant hominum,* Circique *boatus,*
> *Mugitusve Fori; sed me Penetralia veris,*
> *Horroresque trahunt muti, & Consortia sola,*[10]   (ll. 16–19)

not only bears references to the Muses and Apollo but refers also to the Roman Forum, to the bellowing "circus" of sycophants who attached themselves to the great. Of all this no mention is made in the revised poem. Again, the fourth stanza of "The Garden" is highly compressed in comparison with the corresponding part of the Latin text. During revision Marvell cut out half of the mythological allusions, trimming seventeen lines to eight. As we can see, /157/

> *Hic Amor, exutis crepidatus inambulat alis,*
> *Enerves arcus & stridula tela reponens,*
> *Invertitque faces, nec se cupit usque timeri;*
> *Aut exporrectus jacet, indormitque pharetrae;*
> *Non auditurus quanquam Cytherea vocarit;*
> *Nequitias referunt nec somnia vana priores.*
>   *Laetantur* Superi, *defervescente Tyranno,*
> *Et licet experti toties* Nymphasque Deasque,
> Arbore *nunc melius potiuntur quisque cupita.*
> Jupiter *annosam, neglecta conjuge,* Quercum
> Deperit; *haud alia doluit sic pellice* Juno.
> Lemniacum *temerant vestigia nulla Cubile,*
> Nec Veneris Mavors *meminit si* Fraxinus *adsit.*
> *Formosae pressit* Daphnes *vestigia* Phaebus
> *Ut fieret* Laurus; *sed nil quaesiverat ultra.*
> *Capripes & peteret quòd* Pan Syringa *fugacem,*
> *Hoc erat ut* Calamum *posset reperire Sonorum*   (ll. 32–48)

is hardly the Latin equivalent of

> When we have run our Passions heat,
> Love hither makes his best retreat.
> The *Gods,* that mortal Beauty chase,
> Still in a Tree did end their race.
> *Apollo* hunted *Daphne* so,
> Only that She might Laurel grow.
> And *Pan* did after *Syrinx* speed,
> Not as a Nymph, but for a Reed.

The comment of Marvell's first editor following the above seventeen Latin lines—"Desunt multa"—must be seen as something more than a little suspect. There is no evidence that anything is "missing" from "Hortus." The differences between the two poems (in the absence of a complete manuscript of "Hortus") must be explained as the result of the author's revision. This would seem a fortiori true since the four stanzas added to the English poem most markedly depart from the earlier Latin sequence. If this is so, clearly any attempt to explicate "The Garden" by ascertaining the sense of the Latin poem must fail. It happens that where the poems most dramatically diverge Marvell's revision identifies the context in which "The Garden" should be understood, and this context is not relevant to the Latin poem at all.[11] For this reason, when King attempts to gloss the English poem by imposing on the English /158/ word the nuance of the Latin usage, he begs the question. There is no such thing as a "meaning" of any word outside a given linquistic context. And where the context changes, so often does the "meaning"; when the context changes, so often do the function and tone of the "same" word. When these English stanzas are placed in their proper context, we see not only that the tone of the poem changes but that the meaning of the imagery of the poem is radically altered. Finally, when these changes are seen from a proper perspective, most of the difficulties created by modern criticism disappear.

In spite of their differences, on this much critics agree: in Stanza V (where the author's most radical revision begins) the speaker's role is undeniably passive. He may "lead" a "wond'rous Life in" the garden, but it is the fruits of the garden which "drop," "crush," "reach," and the flowers which insnare. True, the speaker falls, but even in falling he remains a passive agent. "Stumbling on Melons" as he passes, he continues to be acted upon by the multiplicity of garden forms. Finally, the flowers of the garden reach out for him, just as had the "Clusters of the Vine." If there is eroticism in this stanza, its strongest impulse is located in the figures—not of nature (the term is too inclusive)—but of the garden. Again, the notion of the speaker's fall into sin implies the exercise of the will. Yet it seems clear that during Stanza V the speaker remains in a passive, receptive state. Though in certain contexts "grass" means "flesh," the word is used here as one of a series of poetic figures, all having parallel functions in expressing the active love of the garden. Thus, the grass provides a comfortable bed for the speaker's "repose." In turn, this repose is both a prerequisite for and a prelude to the experience described in the succeeding stanzas, which are products, also, of the author's revision.

It must be admitted that in one sense both poems deal with eroticism, if we are to use that term in its broadest sense. That is, both poems describe the presence of lovers in the garden, the carving on the trees, the race of the pagan gods for the elusive nymphs. But in the handling of the love motif the greatest difference appears, and here is where the meaning of Marvell's revision begins to be seen. In "The Garden," the plants love man. Not so in "Hortus." In the Latin poem the vegetable world does not move /159/ toward the speaker in any way. Rather, it is as if the garden (almost capriciously) hides Quiet from him:

> *Alma Quies, teneo te! & te Germana Quietis*
> *Simplicitas! Vos ergo diu per Templa, per urbes,*
> *Quaesivi, Regum perque alta Palatia frustra.*
> *Sed vos Hortorum per opaca silentia longe*
> *Celarant Plantae virides, & concolor Umbra.*   (ll. 7–11)

In the revised poem, responsibility for the absence of Quiet belongs to the speaker. And at the same time, the "green plants" (*Plantæ virides*) are elevated to a religious category ("sacred Plants"). Again, whereas in the Latin work the comparison of the trees to the beauty of women is highly detailed, touching the hair, the arms, the voice of the mistress and the leaves, branches, and whispering of the trees, in "The Garden" the qualities of the trees are made much less particular. We are told only that their "Beauties" far exceed those of any mistress. Nor does Stanza V carry through the parallelism of the Latin poem, where the branches of the trees were the passive recipients of the speaker's adoration. Rather, in "The Garden," the trees assume the role of love's aggressor, as they thrust themselves upon a passive speaker.

But in the last analysis we find the best evidence that "The Garden" should be read in the context of the Song of Songs in comparison between Stanza V:

What wond'rous Life in this I lead!
Ripe Apples drop about my head;
The Luscious Clusters of the Vine
Upon my Mouth do crush their Wine;
The Nectaren, and curious Peach,
Into my hands themselves do reach;
Stumbling on Melons, as I pass,
Insnar'd with Flow'rs, I fall on Grass,

and this passage from Casimire:

The Apple ripe drops from its stalke to thee,
    From tast of death made free.
The luscious fruit from the full Figtree shall
    Into thy bosome fall.
Meane while, the Vine no pruning knife doth know,
    The wounded earth no plow.[12]

/160/ In Stanza V, the most radical departure from the Latin origi-
nal, Marvell echoes Casimire's ode, "Out of Solomon's Sacred Mar-
riage Song," which was only one of the many paraphrases of the Song
of Songs available to him. Marvell does more, of course, than merely
borrow the figure of "luscious fruit" falling on a passive speaker,
for indeed that figure is a familiar one within the context of the
Song of Songs. He adds a series of concrete details which suggest,
rather than stipulate, the lusciousness of the garden forms. To be
sure, the ripe apple drops, but now it is only one of many forms,
dropping about the speaker's head. Now, too, the "Clusters of the
Vine" assume a "luscious" quality, as they crush their wine upon
the speaker's lips. The various forms of the garden reach out for the
speaker, give themselves to him in an act of self-immolation. As
many critics have observed, the garden appears almost to pursue
the speaker. Unhappily, about this active love of the garden the
critics have been generally confused.

"A GREEN THOUGHT IN A GREEN SHADE"

It might be argued that even if we allowed for an allegorical inter-
pretation of "The Garden" in terms of the Song of Songs, we should
not have explained the data in the poem. In particular, the bearing
of this view on the passivity of the speaker is not at once clear. To
this we must reply that we have just illuminated that passivity by
identifying the speaker in the poem as the devout soul, who, by
merit of her inclusion in the Mystical Body of the Church, is the
Bride of Christ. In this context, the speaker's passivity is not at all

problematic, for it implies the expected relation between Bride and Bridegroom. Thus, the context of the Canticles would adequately explain the aggressive role of the garden, which pursues, captures, and embraces the Beloved. But would it though? For if the garden is the soul, and if the soul is the Bride of Christ, in what sense may she be pursued by herself? The answer to this question may be easily given, but only insofar as a traditional ambiguity (as distinct from vagueness) of biblical commentary—ambiguity residing in the figure of divine marriage—is understood. In the first chapter, we discussed the way in which the Song of Songs /161/ was believed to describe the three marriages of Christ, two of which are relevant here. The first marriage took place with the quickening and fruitfulness of Mary's womb: the marriage between Word and flesh, for Mary was the Church as well as the Virgin-Mother of God. The second wedding was seen in the Sacrifice, which, like the Virgin Birth, was often represented in the context of hortus conclusus; as the earlier chapters show, above all the imagery of the Song of Songs was eucharistic, since only by partaking of the fruit of Sacrifice was man made secure behind the garden wall of the Mother Church. In this way, man recapitulated the life of Christ in a necessarily dependent role. The splendor of Solomon's wedding, the openly erotic description of physical beauty, the detailed narrative of Love's banquet (Stanza V) —all the richness in the Song of Songs—referred to the inscrutable mystery of the Sacrifice.

Marvell's revision introduces the associated meanings of this context into the poem, and this is nowhere more evident than in his manipulation of the figure of shade. Not that this figure is absent or of no value in the classical "Hortus"; in the second stanza of the Latin work, value is imputed to both shade and the figure "green" (*"Celarant Plantæ virides, & concolor Umbra"*). But note a critical difference. Here, the plant and shade are green; in the revised "Garden," a poem treating of religious ecstacy, greenness is the quality of the speaker's thought. Again, *"concolor Umbra"* is a weak assertion of the color of the shade. It is very clear, if we consider the Latin stanza as a whole, that the emphasis differs greatly from that in the line, "A green Thought in a green Shade." The green plants, linked in the Latin poem to a "like-colored" shade, become in the second stanza of "The Garden" "sacred Plants," while the "like-colored" shade is transmuted to the green dwelling place of "a green Thought." What does this manipulation of color imagery and of the figure of shade mean? It means that Marvell is invoking specifically eucharistic and mystical associations of the image of the garden shade.

It will be helpful here to bear in mind a structural function of Stanza V, which provides the link between the fourth stanza and all that is to follow. This function rests on a feature so simple as to escape notice, namely on Marvell's use of the color green. Cer- /162/ tainly the most debated couplet in the poem ends the sixth stanza: "Annihilating all that's made/ To a green Thought in a green Shade." But though the critics have tended to follow Empson into speculation as to the "meaning" of this annihilation, the best hint as to the meaning of the passage lies in its use of color imagery: Stanza VI is linked to Stanza V by the imagery of shade and the color green. The "Thought" and the "Shade" share the color of the grass on which the speaker has fallen. But another, more subtle, relation holds: the single branches of Oak, Palm, and Laurel are green also. It must be, then, that greenness in itself does not present the final statement of value in the poem. Instead, that value is represented by shade when in conjunction with the color green. Careful reading will show that there are in "The Garden" degrees of shade, and that the system of value developed by the contrasts in the poem is a function of the image of shade. For this reason it is not enough to explain the "meaning" of the item "green"; the meaning of any linguistic item is determined by its context, in this case the allegorical tradition of the Song of Songs. We want to know how the imagery in "The Garden" functions in that context—in short, the contextual meaning of such figures as green, fruit, thought, flame, sun, shade. We want to know, above all, what Marvell means by his governing figure of the garden.

If this analysis is correct, Marvell is drawing on a contrast which is basic to the tradition of the Song of Songs—that between the garden and the not-garden. In iconography, the latter is most often seen as a desert or wilderness. In "The Garden," Marvell develops a series of contrasts which establishes a hierarchy of values. These, in turn, point up the primary and overriding antithesis between the garden and the not-garden. It is not the city and the country which Marvell poses as alternatives here, but shade and its absence, growth and its lack. In the first stanza, the limits of "uncessant Labours" emerge, not simply through contrast between labor and repose, but also by an implied comparison of the effects of the one with those of the other. Men frustrate themselves by seeking the tokens of worldly acclaim, for even when these are achieved they prove to be of little value.

The plain fact is that physical effort leads to a dearth of shade, and therefore to the opposite of value: /163/

> How vainly men themselves amaze
> To win the Palm, the Oke, or Bayes;
> And their uncessant Labours see
> Crown'd from some single Herb or Tree.
> Whose short and narrow verged Shade
> Does prudently their Toyles upbraid;
> While all Flow'rs and all Trees do close
> To weave the Garlands of repose.

The "Toyles" of the men are inextricable from amazement or confusion. Their "uncessant Labours" must be seen as vain. In fact, pathos may be discerned here. The reader is aware that the Palm, the Oak, the Bay are rewards which go only to a limited number of fortunate human beings, to those who are victorious in the various arenas of competition. Yet these rewards, rather than suggesting the satisfactions of power and fame, bear witness to the meaninglessness of even the most effective human effort. For the highest reward the world may endow is a wreath which offers but a "short and narrow verged Shade." Yet it is for such spindly, single branches that the "Companies of Men" endlessly strive. Ironically, the very rewards of worldly success testify to men that their most diligent labors are meaningless, since these rewards cannot produce the one thing of undoubted value: shade. In the garden, where the speaker finds solitude, "all Flow'rs and all Trees do close/ To weave the Garlands of repose." That is, labor and repose are parallel and mutually exclusive functions leading to different and diametrically opposed ends. As early as the first stanza, passivity is linked with a quantity of shade, labor with dearth.

Writers on the Song of Songs had long held the labors of men to be of little value. Man's effort to redeem himself under the Law had proved futile, since no amount of labor could restore him to his lost estate. Since the Law represented the just demands of a righteous God, we often read of the "burning wrath" of its heat. That is why in iconography Adam's labors are pictured in scenes of desolation. He had been shut from the garden of plenty to toil in the blazing sands of the wilderness. Until the advent of Grace (the "shadow

of the sacraments") man was, as we read in Vaughan's "The Search,"
completely at the mercy of nature, wholly dependent on his own
designs.

Thus, in "The Garden," motion and effort are always linked /164/
with heat, whether with the heat of vain, unceasing labors or with the
heat of the race put on by Apollo and Pan for "mortal Beauty":

> When we have run our Passions heat,
> Love hither makes his best retreat.
> The *Gods*, that mortal Beauty chase,
> Still in a Tree did end their race.
> *Apollo* hunted *Daphne* so,
> Only that She might Laurel grow.
> And *Pan* did after *Syrinx* speed,
> Not as a Nymph, but for a Reed.

This stanza introduces another aspect of sexuality to "The Garden."
But certainly Legouis must be mistaken; though a contrapuntal
arrangement exists between Stanzas IV and VIII:

> Such was that happy Garden-state,
> While Man there walk'd without a Mate:
> After a Place so pure, and sweet,
> What other Help could yet be meet!
> But 'twas beyond a Mortal's share
> To wander solitary there:
> Two Paradises 'twere in one
> To live in Paradise alone,

misogyny is not the issue here. Instead, the two stanzas play upon a
theme of solitude, which runs through the entire poem but emerges
now and again with greater emphasis. It should be clear, however,
that the speaker rejects—not woman—but company. Just as he was
earlier misled in his belief that "Fair quiet" and "Innocence" were
to be found among the "Companies of Men," the "Fond Lovers"
remain confused over the proper means to satisfaction and the proper
end of human life. Foolishly they defile the garden, preferring the
passions of the body to the love of God, and so afflict themselves
with "Passions heat." Again, rather than existing in contrast to
the "Fond Lovers," as some have suggested, the pagan gods suffer
the same "cruel" flame, since they, too, are found in hot pursuit
of "mortal Beauty." The pagan gods and lovers alike "run" through
"Passions heat," and in their chase for "mortal Beauty" they suffer

with vain men the heat of frustration. The pagan gods end their race in possession of single branches, the "Fond Lovers" with the cruel heat of their love. /165/

Much has been written about paradox in "The Garden." It seems to me, however, that if paradox exists at all in this poem it is found preeminently in Stanza III, not Stanza V (where critics usually find it). It is paradoxical indeed that, though the idea of love conjures expectations of tenderness, in fact, lovers are cruel:

> No white nor red was ever seen
> So am'rous as this lovely green.
> Fond Lovers, cruel as their Flame,
> Cut in these Trees their Mistress name.
> Little, Alas, they know, or heed,
> How far these Beauties Hers exceed!
> Fair Trees! where s'eer your barkes I wound,
> No Name shall but your own be found.

The flame here refers, of course, to the freezing fire of courtly love, a motif which, as we have seen, was long associated with the garden image. In cutting their mistresses' names on the trees, in distorting the original loveliness of the garden, foolish lovers betray their lack of discernment, and in this way reveal how little they truly know of love's nature. The trees (emblems of divine love and of its productive effects) represent the spiritual potentialities of man, which are more beautiful than the features of any woman. We get some idea of the ironic intent of Marvell's use of the garden image when we recall the allegorical gardens in such works as the *Roman de la Rose*, Nevill's *Castell of Pleasure*, and Beaumont's *Psyche*, where the figure is used to unfold a veritable anatomy of confusion in love. In these works, Solomon's retreat is in either explicit or implicit contrast to the bewildering paradise of natural love. Man is naturally inclined to pursue the overheated pleasures of this world; that is why concupiscence is so often described as flame. But the garden into which man enters for his body's pleasure is distinct from that entered by Marvell's speaker. The poet's irony stems from the juxtaposition of the apparent (or physical) with the essentially true. Caught up in passions that burn, the "Fond" lover, like the protagonists of the *Roman* and *Psyche*, is trapped in a confusing garden from which he cannot escape. But—and here the injunctions of the sundials must be borne in mind—for whatever amazement enters the mind, for whatever humiliation or ultimate defeat must be suffered, for whatever bizarre scene meets /166/ the eye (the vision of carved trees), the will is responsible. With this convention in mind, we are ready to grasp the full impact of the contrast between Stanzas IV and V:

> When we have run our Passions heat,
> Love hither makes his best retreat.
> The *Gods*, that mortal Beauty chase,
> Still in a Tree did end their race.
> *Apollo* hunted *Daphne* so,
> Only that She might Laurel grow.
> And *Pan* did after *Syrinx* speed,
> Not as a Nymph, but for a Reed.
>
> What wond'rous Life in this I lead!
> Ripe Apples drop about my head;
> The Luscious Clusters of the Vine
> Upon my Mouth do crush their Wine;
> The Nectaren, and curious Peach,
> Into my hands themselves do reach;
> Stumbling on Melons, as I pass,
> Insnar'd with Flow'rs, I fall on Grass.

The juxtaposition of Stanzas IV and V presents a vivid contrast between the single branches won by the pagan gods and the opulent garden growth. This contrast points up the difference between the heat of human effort—regardless of what sort—and the shaded repose of the garden, the one represented by single branches, the other by abundant fruit. The lovers and the pagan gods of Stanza IV (the latter with their all-to-human strivings) illustrate the elusive satisfactions of "Passions heat," lending a final picture of the wilderness of human nature, and preparing the reader for a glimpse of the enclosed garden of the Song of Songs.

In Stanza V we have a sequence of figures—drawn from the paraphrases of the Song of Songs—which represent the life-giving power of divine love: the language of the passage is, above all, eucharistic. When the Bride of the Song of Songs exclaimed, "I sate downe under his shadow with great delight, and his fruit was sweete to my taste," she gave voice to her gratitude for the Sacrifice. The tree was the apple tree ("As the apple tree among the trees of the wood, so is my beloved among the sonnes"), which was, in turn, a type of the Cross. In Chapter Three we discussed the dense associations of this figure, which, taken together, meant /167/ Christ was the tree and its fruit also. He was the grapes which crush themselves, for the tree

was a winepress; he was the fruit of the vine, and the liquor distilled
through the Sacrifice. The apples fall in Marvell's poem—of course
they do—just as they had in the "Exposition of the Songs," in *Pia
Desideria,* and in Quarles' *Emblemes* (see our figs. 29-31), and their
falling is a reminder that the Eucharist was freely given in an act
of self-immolation. The speaker's passivity at this stage refers to the
belief that to receive such delicious meat and drink man had but to
"sit still." Thus, we find the Bride sitting beneath the tree, apples
falling all about her, while in the tree her Saviour hangs, crucified.
As in Quarles' emblem, the soul has grasped the eucharsitic meaning
of the tree's shade. In a moment of supreme surrender she has placed
herself at last beyond the reach of the "burning sun of the wrath of
God," which before had given her cause to complain:

> I know not where to go, nor where to stay:
>   The eye of vengeance burnes; her flames invade
>   My sweltring Soule: My soule has oft assaid
> But she can find no shrowd, but she can feele no Shade.[13]

Through meditation, as Prynne had written, the soul unfolds the
mystery of the garden:

> Christ hath *a shade most sweete*
> *Against all scalding Heates, all stormes we meete,*
> *Yea from his Fathers burning Wrath and Rage,*
> *Which none but he can quench, coole, or asswage: . . . ,*[14]

and come to know the shade as the author of her repose:

> *Here may they find, blest rest, repose, and ease,*
> *When nought else can them comfort or appease.*
> O let our soules for ever dwell and rest
> In its refreshing shade, which makes them blest.[15]

Here is protection from the burning sun of the Law, that divine
umbrella which allows Marvell's speaker to refer late in the poem
to "a milder sun." The sun is milder because, by God's Grace, its
effect has been palliated. It is proper that the fruit of the garden
come to the speaker without effort on his part. For the Sacrifice was
brought about by man's own powerlessness to help himself. A gift,
the Eucharist descended upon man without his effort and /168/ re-
gardless of his worth. For if his worth were the measure of his salva-
tion (as during the dispensation of Law it was) man would labor

as endlessly and with as little hope of gain as do the "Companies of Men." The lush quality of the imagery in Stanza V, in contrast to the single branches of Stanza I, stipulates the difference between the state of nature and the state of Grace. It represents the contrast between the limited potentialities of natural man and the limitless power of God.

In this context, even the greenness of the grass unfolds a mystery. The grass where the speaker falls is that "bed of green" on which the matchless love of Bride and Bridegroom is consummated. In the King James version, the Latin "Lectulus noster floridus" was translated "our bedde is greene"; Giovanni Diodati translated the passage "il nostro letto etiando e verdeggiante." According to tradition, the greenness of this bed represented the fruitfulness of Christ's union with the Church, of which Solomon's marriage was a type. It was the sign of regeneration made possible by the eclipse of the sun of the Law; the Christ Tree, the apple tree, shaded man from the Law's condemnation, allowing a garden to spring where all had been desert. The wilderness, emblem of the breach between God and man, belonged to nature, for into nature man had fallen. But as we read in Herbert's "Sunday," at the Sacrifice, Christ enclosed a garden for his pleasure. Thus, T. S. translates "Also our fruitful bed is green," explaining that the bed was that place "*Where Christ conjoyns in spiritual union*," producing "*great increase.*"[16] William Baldwin expresses the same traditional view: "*Beholde our Bed, our peace most plentiful/ Of conscience, doeth flourish through thy myght.*"[17] As we have observed, poetic paraphrases of the Song of Songs lent their full weight to the perpetuation of such typical interpretations. In Gervase Markham's *Poem of Poems* (1596), we read:

> (Dearelie belov'd) double thou art as faire,
> And more than faire pleasure consorts with thee,
> Beautious pleasant; pleasant beautious deare,
> To this thou addest all eternitie;
>   And ever greene our bridall bed shall bee.[18]

The quality of green, in this context, refers to the flourishing of the bed where Christ and his Bride are joined in marriage. The /169/ block book *Canticum Canticorum* illustrates this idea, with its bed covered with roses (our fig. 33), and this iconographic example resembles a passage in Baldwin, where we read, "Our bed is decked with flowers." The same idea emerges in such Flemish paintings as Roger van der Weyden's "Annunciation" (fig. 4).[19] Earlier, we discussed the way in which the Annunciation functioned in the iconography of Speculum, linked in almost every instance with the enclosed garden of the Song of Songs (figs. 4, 5, and 17). In such paintings the artist drew upon the exegetical tradition which held that Mary was the first Bride of Christ, hortus conclusus of the Church, and paradigm of the devout soul. As the wall enclosing the flowers of the Elect from the weeds of the damned, Mary became, in her role as the Church, a model of the individual soul, who, as the "living stone" from which the walls of the Temple were built, was an enclosed garden in microcosm. Thus, the touchstone of the enclosed garden as an emblem (*hortus mentis*) of man's inner being. This is how the figure was used by St. Teresa and St. John, and how it was used by Herbert, Vaughan, and Marvell.

As we may see from comparison with dozens of paraphrases of the Song of Songs, Marvell is writing of the shadow of the apple tree, where the Spouse reclines in full enpoyment of the "shade of Grace." In this shadow, the soul transcends the limitations of human nature; there and only there does she flourish in virtue. In the shadow of the Christ-Tree, the Bride of the Song finds a "bed of green," where she enjoys the full delight of spiritual union. This is that delicious "repose," that ineffable passivity described by St. Teresa. As we read in Chapter Three, unfolding the true sense of that mysterious Scripture, "I sat down under the shadow of him whom I desired and his fruit is sweet to my palate," she wrote: "A person in this state has no need, for any purpose, to move her hand, or to rise (I mean by this to practise meditation), for the Lord is giving her the fruit from the apple-tree with which she compares her Beloved: He picks it and cooks it and almost eats it for her."[20] As in Marvell's poem, the fruit comes to the speaker without effort, since the aim of meditation has been achieved: "For here all is enjoyment, without any labour of the faculties"; moreover, "While the soul is enjoying the delight which /170/ has been described, it seems to be wholly engulfed and protected by a shadow."

We are now in a better position to consider the structural function of Stanza V, which precedes this highly problematic stanza:

> Mean while the Mind, from pleasure less,
> Withdraws into its happiness:
> The Mind, that Ocean where each kind
> Does streight its own resemblance find;
> Yet it creates, transcending these,
> Far other Worlds, and other Seas;

> Annihilating all that's made
> To a green Thought in a green Shade.

Critics have often asked what Marvell meant by "pleasure less." While this is an interesting question, another seems to me to be more profitably advanced: What is the sense of "Mean while"? This is a convenient question because, as a glance at Casimire will show, Marvell's model uses the term in a manner clearly synonymous with "all the while." In other words, "Mean while," or during the speaker's sojourn in the garden (and perhaps even longer), "the Vine no pruning knife doth know,/ The wounded earth no plow." All this may seem too simple, but the point may help explain Marvell's figure of withdrawal, and thereby place Stanzas V and VI in a meaningful relation to the first four stanzas (which, we must remember, have been viewed by critics as being somehow cut off from them). In Casimire's poem, the speaker is saying that the mystical garden has prospered for a great length of time by supernatural means. Similarly, the mind of Marvell's speaker has been withdrawing from the moment of his entrance into the temporal garden. In Stanza VI, following successful meditation, his mind is elevated, his affections moved. As we read in St. Teresa, the soul has no further need of meditation. The significance of the temporal object has been understood, the analogy between the garden and the potentiality of the soul recognized. Now the goal of meditation—the contemplative state—has been achieved. In that state, such handbooks as *The Mind's Road to God* or *The Spiritual Canticle* insist, the soul finds the closest approximation possible in this life to that union for which the enclosed garden of the Song of Songs is the emblem. /171/

Now, the images of green and shade converge. The speaker's thought (or state of mind) is the purest expression—the fruition— of the devout life, which is, in turn, the desideratum of the dispensation of Grace. In this state is the highest expression of spiritual ascent; the "sacred Plants" of "Fair quiet" and "Innocence" (the issue, now, of meditation) flourish in what many of Marvell's contemporaries and literary progenitors had come to think of as the "shade of Grace." It may appear that such a comment derives from an excessive reading back of later upon earlier stanzas. But this is not the case, for the image of shade has functioned powerfully throughout the earlier stanzas of "The Garden." The "sacred Plants" are those "flowers of virtue" sought by the saints as the desired end product of meditation. And they grow "Only among the Plants," only in the solitude of the garden of meditation, what Casimire

called in Marvell's model poem "the sacred Green." As "The Gar-
den" unfolds, the reader learns that the alternative to "uncessant
Labours" is not idleness; the speaker's passivity must not be con-
fused with sloth.[21] /171/

COMPUTING TIME

/176/ Clearly, the four stanzas added to "The Garden" require and
clarify our rereading of the earlier ones, regardless, now, of the latter's
/177/ similarity to parts of "Hortus." Such rereading, in turn, illumi-
nates the revised portions. In the context of the Song of Songs, the
early stanzas (I-IV) concern the movement of the soul from sensitive
perception of a physical object *toward* the state for which that object
traditionally stands. The earlier stanzas are now seen as the prelim-
inary stages of meditation, where the soul discovers the application
of the garden to human conduct. The insight gained at this (moral)
level corresponds to the tropological meaning of Scripture, and rep-
resents the first departure of the soul from the literal understanding
of Creation. Immediately following this new awareness comes the
meaning of the object with reference to the speaker's own soul; in
the de contemptu mundi tradition, the soul apprehends its mistaken
pursuit of worldly values (II) and ponders the general folly of
others (III–IV). Finally, the soul ends its allegorical rumination;
as in Prynne's "Christian Paradise," the garden has painted before
the speaker's eyes the figure of the crucified Christ. Of course Stanza
V is ambiguous, but not necessarily because of any sexual attitude
Marvell did or did not have. Within the context of the Song of
Songs, this ambiguity is a traditional aspect of the language, deriving
from the possible juxtaposition of allegorical and anagogical levels
of meaning for exactly the same pattern of images: the image-cluster
of the enclosed garden. Not only do the eucharastic figures of tree,
fruit, and shade suggest the riches of Love's banquet, they shadow
forth the mysteries of spiritual union as they were known in their
highest, experiential form.

As the mystics write, in this highest of all possible conditions it is
as if the soul has departed from the body:

> Here at the Fountains sliding foot,
> Or at some Fruit-trees mossy root,
> Casting the Bodies Vest aside,
> My Soul into the boughs does glide:
> There like a Bird it sits, and sings,
> Then whets, and combs its silver Wings;

> And, till prepar'd for longer flight,
> Waves in its Plumes the various Light.

Apparently, the "Here" refers to the preceding stanzas, which describe the shaded garden bed where the speaker has fallen. In /178/ experience, the speaker has meditated on the object of his love in such a way as to have become momentarily fused with it. The soul, in its active capacity, "glides" into the boughs of the tree in whose shade it has flourished. This gliding movement (an invention of the author's revision) represents a logical development of the two preceding stanzas, and indeed of the preceding poem as a whole, with its movement *toward* the anagogic or mystical level of meaning. At last, it seems as if the body has disappeared, as if all the universe has merged with the object of the speaker's contemplation. As in figure 34, the speaker's entire being has ascended into the tree, to become wholly separated from the world. In this miniature, a monk (lover of "delicious Solitude") retreats from the world, which stretches beneath him as a dualism between light and dark; on our right, a huge black rat and the open jaws of a wide-eyed beast are in contrast to the peaceful unicorn, the white rat, and the general brightness of the opposite side of the painting. As in Marvell's "Garden," the contrasts here reflect the potentiality of withdrawal from the world. And here, as in the "Zacheus" poems of Quarles, man climbs the physical tree in Imitatio Christi, and in so doing ascends the ladder of perfection.

This is what Marvell means by his figure of annihilation. As we saw in Chapter Four, in John Hall's "Emblem 14" (drawn from Augustine's text, "I will pierce heaven with my mind, and be present with thee in my desires") the subject is the exertion of the will directing love toward heaven. The point of that example is worth repeating. In the Hall emblem divine Cupid aims an arrow at heaven, as another already bends upon striking the blazing heart of God's love. Nearby, the Spouse sits in her usually passive position. The soul in her role as Spouse becomes aware of an expansion, as if she would become an "Ocean where each kind/ Does streight its own resemblance find":

> Swell heart into a world and keep
> That humid sea:
> Become, my bosome, one great deep
> That it may lodge in Thee:
> That glorious sun with his Celestiall heat
> will warm't, and mak't evaporate.[22]

/179/ The heart swells, becoming more and more amenable to the
rays of God's love, until finally all division between the object and
that love has disappeared:

> Spring-head of life, how am I now
> Intomb'd in Thee?
> How do I since th' art pleas'd to flow,
> Hate a dualitie?
> How I am annihilated? yet by this
> Acknowledge my subsistence is.

The speaker is "Intomb'd" because he had died to the present
world. Hating all division from its true essence, which is spiritual
and therefore divine, the soul rises from one moment in time into
the timeless:

> Still may I rise; still further clime
> Till that I lie
> (Having out-run-short-winded time)
> Swath'd in Eternitie.[23]

Critics rightly point to the death motif in Stanza VII of "The
Garden." The "longer flight" refers to that ultimate separation of
soul and body (the two are apart now only momentarily), which
transpires only once "That subtile knot, which makes us man"
has been forever untied. Of course, the mere fact that a shorter flight
is in progress testifies to the regenerative process which has taken
place, and which the garden represents. This is the meaning of
Vaughan's allusion to hortus conclusus in "Regeneration." However,
whereas Vaughan's speaker had heard the whispering of the wind
in the mystical garden (assurance of regeneration and sign that the
highest level of experience has been achieved), now Marvell's speaker
feels himself divested of his clothing of flesh, as if the knot of human-
ity with all its restrictions has already been undone. He feels a
motion in his soul, as of a bird gliding into the branches of the soul's
beloved tree. Once perched in its boughs, the bird sends forth a
song of reciprocal love. We recall, of course, how springtime in the
Song of Songs was heralded by the "time of the singing of birds,"
notably, by "the voice of the turtle." The dove, represented in
Hawkins' emblem of the enclosed garden, appears also in Speculum,
bearing the sprig of olive to the ark as /180/ a reminder of God's
mercy. Perhaps, as in the paraphrases, this is the bird which "sits" in
the tree "and sings":

> the flowrs appear shew summer's near
> Each chirping bird doth sit and sing,
> The turtles voice doth make a noise,
> All which bespeak a glorious spring.[24]

Meditation, the primary source of movement in the garden, is the crux for the exercise of the will. Of course, this point immediately suggests another familiar implication of the bird image: meditation is itself a bird on whose wings the soul is lofted into union with the divine essence: the soul, animated by a desire "to give it selfe to the beloved object," is drawn as on "the winge of the dove, to flie to her repose, . . . [to] her beloved."[25] As we saw in Stanza IX, the alternative to "uncessant Labours" is not sloth but spiritual industry. The annihilation of time and the objects of time is predicated on the proper exercise of the soul, which resembles the profitable employment of the bee:

> How well the skilful Gardner drew
> Of flow'rs and herbes this Dial new;
> Where from above the milder Sun
> Does through a fragrant Zodiack run;
> And, as it works, th' industrious Bee
> Computes its time as well as we.
> How could such sweet and wholsome Hours
> Be reckon'd but with herbs and flow'rs!

As the emblem tradition would have it, the bee presents man with an emblem of the proper way of counting (computing, spending) time. He is, as Wither writes, "laborious in an honest way,"[26] neither idle nor unceasing in his work. As Marvell's figure of the floral sundial reminds the reader, Time presents man with the choice of how to spend his time. If he is wise, he emulates the bee. For, in the last analysis, asks John Wall,

> What is the Church but as a garden? What are we but as spirituall Bees?
> O let us sucke the flowers and draw the sweetnesse, and never rest, till
> we have made a hive of our soules and bodies: that our hearts may be
> as waxe, softened, and mollified, for the impression of this seale, and
> nothing but this.[27]

/181/ And as St. François de Sales writes, where is the spiritual bee led in meditation except to those divine passions described in the Song of Songs?

Thus the celestiall Spouse, as a mysticall bee, flies to the Canticle of
Canticles, now upon the eyes, now upon the lippes, cheekes and head
haire of the well-beloved, to draw from thence the sweetnesse of a
thousand passions of love; . . . .[28]

Emulating the profitable employment of the bee, man makes a
proper use of the temporal garden, employing it as setting for and
emblem of meditation (see fig. 41). Because of this, he escapes the
blazing sun of God's justice, which, in the state of nature—indepen-
dent of Grace—prevails. Again, Marvell's revision was accomplished
within the allegorical tradition of the Song of Songs. The Latin
"candidior" becomes "milder," the new form suggesting that the
effect of the sun in "The Garden" bears not only upon the sight
but upon all those parts of man's being which are capable of perceiv-
ing either the sun's mildness or its lack. In the context of the Song
of Songs, the mildness refers to the intervention of God's mercy, to
the "shade of Grace" in which the speaker safely dwells. Because his
time has been well spent in solitary meditation, the speaker "com-
putes" his "time" in the manner of the bee, responding to the
garden, which, as Prynne writes, "paints" before his eyes the figure
of Christ, which "tenders" to his "thoughts" the "Soule-ravishing,/
Sweete, heavenly Meditations which doe spring/ From Gardens."[29]
The soul is lifted "high on *Contemplation's* Wings"[30] "Above the
Spheares in a delightfull Trance."[31] Longing for that ultimate union
which the garden typifies, the soul glides into the tree whose shadow
(like a heavenly embrace) is a "milder Sun."

Notes

1 For the view that all literature is "more or less allegorical," see Angus
  Fletcher, *Allegory: The Theory of a Symbolic Mode* (Ithaca, 1964), Intro.
2 For some idea of the range of critical opinion, see Harold Wendell Smith,
  "Cowley, Marvell, and the Second Temple," *Scrutiny*, XIX (1953), 184–
  205; Anthony Hecht, "Shades of Keats and Marvell," *The Hudson Re-
  view*, XV (1962), 50–71. Briefly stated, Hecht sees the subject of both
  poems as "an exquisite secular and sensuous ecstasy . . . which is self-
  induced and autoerotic." See also Pierre Legouis, *André Marvell: poète,
  puritain, patriote* (Paris: Henri Didier, 1928), pp. 123 ff; William
  Empson, "Marvell's 'Garden'," *Scrutiny*, I (1932), 236–40 (this essay is
  included as a chapter in *English Pastoral Poetry* (New York, 1938),
  pp. 119 ff.); A. H. King, "Some Notes on Andrew Marvell's Garden," *ES*,
  XX (1938), 118–21; Milton Klonsky, "A Guide through the Garden," *SR*,
  LVIII (1950), 16–35; M. C. Bradbrook and M. G. Lloyd Thomas, *Andrew*

Marvell (Cambridge, 1940), pp. 59–64; Ruth Wallerstein, *Seventeenth-Century Poetic* (Madison, 1950), pp. 319–35; Frank Kermode, "The Argument of Marvell's 'Garden'," *EC*, II (1952), 225–40; Pierre Legouis, "Marvell and the New Critics," *RES*, VIII (1957), 382–89; Lawrence Hyman, "Marvell's Garden," *ELH*, XXV (1958), 13–22; Maren-Sofie Røstvig, "Andrew Marvell's 'The Garden': A Hermetic Poem," *ES*, XL (1959), 65–76. See also Miss Røstvig's "Benlowes, Marvell, and the Divine Casimire," *HLQ*, XVIII (1954), 13–35, to which I am greatly indebted; Geoffrey H. Hartman, "Marvell, St. Paul, and the Body of Hope," *ELH*, XXXI (1964), 175–94; Harold E. Toliver, *Marvell's Ironic Vision* (New Haven, 1965), pp. 88 ff., 138–51, et passim.

3 René Wellek and Austin Warren, *Theory of Literature* (New York, 1956), p. 31.

4 Wallerstein, pp. 319–40. The reader will recognize my indebtedness to Miss Wallerstein; my differences with her will be equally clear throughout the chapter.

5 Don Cameron Allen, *Image and Meaning* (Baltimore, 1960), ch. 6.

6 Ibid., ch. 7.

7 Røstvig, "Andrew Marvell's 'The Garden': A Hermetic Poem," *ES*, XL (1959), 65–76.

8 Bodleian MS. Fairfax 40, p. 443, quoted by permission of the Bodleian Library, Oxford. A small portion of Fairfax's paraphrase appears in *The Poems of Thomas Third Lord Fairfax*, ed. by Edward Bliss Reed (New Haven, 1909), pp. 259–60.

9 Marvell, *Poems & Letters*, I, 219.

10 For a translation of "Hortus," see the Appendix.

11 For another point of view, see George Williamson, "The Context of Marvell's 'Garden'," *MLN*, LXXVI (1961), 590–98.

12 Casimire Sarbiewski, *The Odes of Casimire*, tr. by G. Hils (1646), pp. 83–89. I am indebted to Miss Røstvig, who first pointed out the connection between Sarbiewski and Marvell in "Benlowes, Marvell, and the Divine Casimire," *HLQ*, XVIII (1954), 13–35, and in *The Happy Man: Studies in the Metamorphoses of a Classical Ideal, 1600–1700* (Oslo, 1954), I, 240–66, esp. p. 259. In relation to "The Garden," Miss Røstvig emphasizes the influence of the *Hermetica*; cf. the argument of the present chapter with her "Andrew Marvell's 'The Garden': A Hermetic Poem," *ES*, XL (1959), 65–76.

13 Francis Quarles, *Emblemes*, p. 237. Again, the lusciousness of the scene draws upon such examples as this from John Davies' *The Muses Sacrifice* (1612):

> O! juycie *Bunch* of *Soule*-refreshing *grapes*,
> > (hard pressed in the *Wine-presse* of the *Crosse!*)
> Make druncke my thirstie *Soule*, that (gasping) gapes
> > for thy pure bloud, to purge mine, being to grosse.
>
> > > > > > > (fol. 22)

14 William Prynne, "A Christian Paradise," in *Mount Orgueil* (1641), p. 124.

15 Ibid., p. 136.

16 T. S., *The Book of the Song of Solomon in Meeter* (1676), p. 4. See Don Cameron Allen, "Symbolic Color in the Literature of the English Renaissance," *PQ*, XV (1936), 81–92.

17 William Baldwin, *The Canticles or Balades of Salomon* (1549), sig. B4.

18 Gervase Markham, *The Poem of Poems* [1596], sig. B4.

19 This painting, now hanging in the New York Metropolitan Museum, depicts an interior Annunciation. The bed in the right half of the painting is covered with roses. Through the window we may see an enclosed garden, and at a distance the Tower of David, with its gate now opened.

20 St. Teresa, *Conceptions of the Love of God*, in *Complete Works*, II, 389.

21 Here I must take strong exception to Hecht, who writes that "the joke at the expense of labor is very lightly stated, and [that] if the poet seems to be recommending a kind of sloth, it is sanctified by nature." Hecht, "Shades of Keats and Marvell," *The Hudson Review*, XV (1962), 51.

22 John Hall, *Emblems With elegant Figures* [1658], p. 53.

23 Ibid., p. 54.

24 T. S., *The Book of the Song of Solomon in Meeter*, p. 6.

25 St. François de Sales, *A Treatise of the Love of God*, tr. by Miles Car (Douay, 1630), p. 373.

26 George Wither, *A Collection of Emblemes*, p. 250.

27 John Wall, *Alae Seraphicae* (1627), p. 24.

28 St. François de Sales, *A Treatise of the Love of God*, p. 328.

29 Prynne, p. 117.

30 In a pastorial dedication to Drummond, Lauder uses the phrase in his description of poetic ecstasy. *The Poetical Works of William Drummond*, ed. by L. E. Kastner (Edinburgh: William Blackwood and Sons, 1913), I, cxii.

31 Prynne, p. 117.

Questions

Stanley N. Stewart's book *The Enclosed Garden* traces an intellectual and literary tradition for the *hortus conclusus* in preparation for the analysis of Marvell's "The Garden" included here. Stewart's basic procedure may be compared with Kermode's. A tradition, primarily yet not exclusively literary, similar to yet broader than our conventional understanding of *genre*, is described and documented. Stewart argues that the allegory of "The Garden" reflects back on the tradition from which the poem developed—that is, on "Solomon's Song."

This selection from Stanley Stewart's book represents in a way a critical composite of earlier methods for proving the views of other writers. For example, can you see the similarity between Maren-Sofie Røstvig's treatment of Fairfax's translations and Stewart's use of these facts?

Do you find Mr. Stewart's context of the Song of Songs more or less helpful than Wallerstein's less specific "Christian Neo-Platonism"? In what ways is Stewart's response to Miss Wallerstein's book similar to Klonsky's?

Will you accept, as an undocumented convenience, the suggestion that "Hortus" was written about a year before "The Garden" (Stewart's essay, p. 156)? Why is this assumption necessary for Stewart's argument?

Does this selection convince you that "The Garden" is an allegorical poem?

J. B. Leishman

The Garden*

Nowhere is that balance between the conceptual and the visual, between the dialectical and the pictorial or descriptive, which is so characteristic of Marvell, more perfectly exemplified than in *The Garden,* which, it seems reasonable to suppose, was composed about the same time as *Appleton House.* But while *Appleton House* is primarily a descriptive poem, *The Garden* is primarily an argumentative or dialectical one; and, since the argument which it develops has recently received much attention, often, as it seems to me, with insufficient observance of that balance between seriousness and light-heartedness which distinguishes the poem, and also with some failure to perceive what other seventeenth-century poems *The Garden* does and does not resemble, it may be as well to begin with some prose (and perhaps rather prosaic) analysis of the nine stanzas in which Marvell has arranged his octo-syllabic couplets.

I.   Those who toil for military, civic or poetic honours are crowned only with the leaves of a single tree (palm, oak or bay), but here all the flowers and all the trees offer us the garlands of repose.

II.   Only here are innocence and quiet to be found. Their plants, unlike those which supply the garlands of ambition, are given only in the places where they grow. Society, in comparison with this delicious solitude, is merely barbarous.

III.   This lovely green excites more desire than the white and red in any woman's cheeks, but lovers, if they will, carve their mistress's name on these trees that so excel her in beauty: the only names I will ever carve on them shall be their own.

---

*Reprinted from *The Art of Marvell's Poetry.* London: Hutchinson & Co., 1966, pp. 292-97, 303-12, by permission of the publisher.

IV.   Apollo only pursued Daphne in order that she might turn into
a laurel, and Pan Syrinx in order that she might turn into a reed.
V.   Fruits offer themselves to me and flowers ensnare me. /293/
VI.   But my mind withdraws from the lesser pleasures of the senses
into that happiness which is within itself, and there, transcending
those external objects that are mirrored within it as terrestrial things
are counterparted in the ocean, it creates other worlds and rejects all
the visible creation in favour of those green, innocent and primal
thoughts that come to it in a green shade.
VII.   My soul leaves the body and glides like a bird into the trees,
where it prepares itself for yet longer flight.
VIII.   Such was the state of Adam in Paradise, before the creation
of Eve. That, however, was a state of happiness too great for a mortal,
and he was not allowed to enjoy it for long.
IX.   How could such hours be reckoned but by a sundial made of
flowers and herbs?

With conscious paradox and hyperbole, with an inimitable com-
bination of jest and earnest, seriousness and light-heartedness, Mar-
vell is here maintaining at least four more or less paradoxical
propositions:

(1) The superiority of the contemplative to the active life.
(2) The superiority, because more favourable to contemplation, of
     solitude to society.
(3) The superiority, for the same reason, of the beauty of gardens
     to the beauty of women.
(4) The superiority of the invisible to the visible and of the inner
     world created by the mind to the external world perceived
     by the senses.

The argument of his poem might also be expressed, less abstractly,
as follows: the only perfect human life we know of was that of Adam,
before the creation of Eve; but through weakly yielding to her
charm he sinned and fell. While Adam was alone, his only sensual
or sensuous pleasures were the sight and smell and taste of flowers
and fruits, and these could not distract him from, nay, rather their
very mildness and unwithholdingness left him free, impelled him to
seek, the higher pleasure of conversing with God.
    In an interesting and stimulating essay on 'The Argument of
Marvell's "Garden" '[1] Professor Frank Kermode seems to me to reveal
an insufficient awareness of what, when all deductions and qualifi-

---

[1] In *Essays in Criticism*, II, no. 3 (July 1952), 225 ff.

cations have been made, I may call the uniqueness of Marvell's poem, and, at the same time, to make far too much of an antithesis, /294/ based on superficial or imaginary resemblances, between what he would have us regard as two *genres* of seventeenth-century poetry: poems in which gardens are praised as places apt for love, and poems in which they are praised as places apt for contemplation. For, while poems, or passages in poems, praising gardens as places apt for love are as old as the *Roman de la Rose,* as old as Petronius (*dignus amore locus*), the first poem distinguishably and memorably celebrating what Professor Kermode would call the Philosopher's Garden is Marvell's. The chief source of what seems to me the errors and confusions in Professor Kermode's essay is probably the fact that he, like some other writers upon Marvell, has persuaded himself that, because Fairfax translated it, Saint-Amant's poem *La Solitude* must have exerted a far greater influence upon Marvell's poetry than it actually did, and that it is far more like Marvell's poetry than it really is.[2] I have already insisted on the fundamental differences between *La Solitude* and *Appleton House* and upon the fact that the only significant resemblance between them is that they may both be regarded as what I have called 'catalogues of delights'. But between *La Solitude* and *The Garden* even that resemblance is absent, and the only link between the two poems is that the word 'solitude' occurs in both. *The Garden* is not, like *La Solitude,* a catalogue of delights, and *La Solitude* is not, like *The Garden,* an argument. *La Solitude* is in no sense argumentative or dialectical, but essentially evocative and romantic, and consists, as I have said, 'of a loosely related series of leisurely and expansively described scenes and images which a mood may "feed upon" '. On the other hand, between *The Garden* and *Appleton House* there are some real affinities, and stanzas from the shorter poem might well have been incorporated at various places in the longer one. Nevertheless, while there are certain dialectical or argumentative passages in *Appleton House*, passages in

---

[2] The first writer to suggest that Marvell's poetry had been influenced by Saint-Amant's seems to have been Edward Bliss Reed, in an article on 'The Poems of Thomas Fairfax', *Transactions of the Connecticut Academy of Arts and Sciences,* XIV, July 1909, 237–90. Assuming that Marvell wrote all (or most) of his 'nature' poems at Nunappleton, Reed declared: 'That these poems were inspired not only by the beauty of Nunappleton, but by its owner's love and appreciation of poetry, there can be little doubt. We may go even further, and see in Marvell's nature-poems some hints from Saint-Amant. Marvell's verse is richer and deeper; where Saint-Amant is vague in his descriptions or conventional in his thought, Marvell is concrete and original; for it is the Englishman, and not the Frenchman, who uses *le mot précis,* and yet Saint-Amant's theme—to lose oneself in Nature—is the theme of *The Garden* and of the finest lines in *Appleton House*' (p. 248).

which the visual and the conceptual, the dialectical and /295/ the descriptive, are combined in much the same way as in *The Garden*, *Appleton House* still remains primarily a descriptive poem, a catalogue of delights, while in *The Garden* description is throughout subordinated to argument, is essentially illustrative. I say 'subordinated to argument', although it is probable that for most readers, who delightedly encounter it for the first time in *The Golden Treasury*, *The Garden* seems primarily a descriptive poem, and that the chief impression it leaves upon them is a pictorial or visual one. It is, I think, above all the purely descriptive and visual fifth stanza, which stands in the exact middle of the poem (four stanzas before it and four after it), that has contributed to produce this, for many readers, abiding impression:

> What wond'rous Life is[3] this I lead!
> Ripe Apples drop about my head;
> The Luscious Clusters of the Vine
> Upon my Mouth do crush their Wine;
> The Nectaren, and curious Peach,
> Into my hands themselves do reach;
> Stumbling on Melons, as I pass,
> Insnar'd with Flow'rs, I fall on Grass.

This stanza, it seems worth remarking, is strikingly reminiscent of some lines (by which it may well have been suggested) in one of the most notable descriptions of a *locus amoenus* in ancient poetry, that passage at the end of Theocritus's seventh Idyl (The Harvest-home) which describes how the three wayfarers, having reached Phrasidamus's farm, lay down on beds of rushes and vine leaves in a place where poplars and elms murmured overhead, a spring flashed near by, and the air was filled with the sound of cicadas and tree-frogs, larks and finches, doves and bees:

All nature smelt of the opulent summer-time, smelt of the season of fruit. Pears lay at our feet, apples on either side rolling abundantly, and the young branches lay splayed upon the ground because of the weight of their damsons.[4]

---

[3] 'Is this': to this Thompson (1776, III 413), with or without MS authority, silently emended the 'in this' of 1681, an emendation accepted (silently again) by Grosart and several other modern editors. I cannot but think that 'is this' must be the authentic reading, and I cannot imagine any really convincing defence of the appropriateness of 'in this'.

[4] ll. 143–6, Loeb translation.

It is, I think, mainly because of the Theocritean glow and colour /296/
radiated from this motionless centre of the poem that many (perhaps
most) readers of *The Garden* fail to perceive, or perhaps only come
to perceive much later, that there is an argument continuously pro-
gressing beneath a surface of description. Marvell, one might almost
say, is arguing in images. In fact, the more closely one considers his
poem, the more deeply aware one becomes, both in manner and in
matter, of its uniqueness.

If it is to be classified at all, it belongs to two often overlapping
genres, the 'Replies' and the 'Paradoxes'. As a Reply it cannot,
indeed, like Crashaw's *Answer for Hope* in reply to Cowley's *Against
Hope* or Strode's *Against Melancholy* in reply to Fletcher's 'Hence,
all you vaine Delights', be regarded as a reply to any particular poem,
but only as a general reply to those innumerable poems and pass-
ages in poems which, from the time of Petronius, had celebrated
either the garden or the *locus amoenus* as a *dignus amore locus*. As a
Paradox, it would seem to be, even in the most restricted and popu-
lar sense of that term, essentially original; for, so far as I am aware,
neither the central paradox, the superiority of solitude to society
(as distinct from the superiority of country life to that of the city
or the court, a well-established Horatian and Virgilian theme that
can scarcely be regarded as paradoxical), nor the subsidiary para-
dox, the superiority of natural to feminine beauty, had ever been
poetically elaborated before. Generations of poets had declared that
the white and red of roses was nothing in comparison with the white
and red in their mistress's cheeks, but no poet before Marvell had
ventured to declare that

> No white nor red was ever seen
> So am'rous as this lovely green.[5]

---

[5] Similarly, it seems likely that many poets before Marvell had declared that it
was cruel of lovers to carve their mistresses' names on trees: Mrs Katherine Philips
('the Matchless Orinda') certainly did so in a poem written long before Marvell's
poems were printed, 'Upon the Graving of her Name upon a Tree in Barn-Elms
Woods' (*Caroline Poets*, ed. Saintsbury, I 583):
> Alas, how barbarous are we,
> Thus to reward the courteous Tree,
> Who its broad shade affording us,
> Deserves not to be wounded thus!
> See how the yielding bark complies
> With our ungrateful injuries!
> And seeing this, say how much then
> Trees are more generous than men,
> Who by a nobleness so pure,
> Can first oblige, and then endure.

/297/ Nevertheless, the manner (as distinct from the matter) of this
subsidiary paradox of Marvell's may be compared with Donne's

> I can love her, and her, and you and you,
> I can love any, so she be not true,[6]

or

> Love built on beauty, soone as beauty, dies,
> Chuse this face, chang'd by no deformities.[7]

Since, however, Marvell's poem is not merely a paradoxical pane-
gyric on solitude but a celebration of the State of Innocence, it is
possible (though not absolutely necessary) to establish connections
between it and the very earliest records of our cultural and religious
inheritance. For the Christian and Old Testament conception of the
State of Innocence, of the unfallen Adam, has affinities with the
ancient Greek and Roman conception of a Golden Age. /303/

Marvell's *Garden*, celebrating—not unseriously, and yet not wholly
seriously, but with much conscious paradox and hyperbole—on the
one hand, the Christian and Old Testament Age of Innocence and,
on the other hand, the superiority of solitude to society, including
the society of women, may indeed be incidentally regarded, and may
well have been incidentally intended, as a reply to these various neo-
classical celebrations of the Golden Age as the Age of Free Love and
of Gardens and other *loci amoeni* as places 'apt for love'. It should,
however, be regarded primarily as a continuation, with much of the
conscious paradox and hyperbole which distinguishes so many seven-
teenth-century poetic debates for and against Inconstancy, Melan-
choly, 'Fruition', Hope, and so forth, of that very ancient philosophic
and theological debate on the respective benefits of society and
solitude, the active and the contemplative life. This debate is at
least as old as *Plato*, who in the *Republic* declared that the philoso-
pher must be compelled, by the penalty of being ruled by men worse
than himself, to forsake from time to time the supreme pleasure of

---

Marvell, though (and here it seems unlikely that he had any predecessor) went
one better, and added:
> Fair trees! where s'eer your barkes I wound,
> No Name shall but your own be found.

Cleveland also had something of this capacity to go one better, to keep the ball
longer in the air, but he seldom exercised it with Marvell's tact and taste.

[6] *The Indifferent*, ll. 8–9.

[7] *Elegie II (The Anagram)*, ll. 27–8.

contemplation in order to take his turn in governing the state. The Stoics in the main followed Plato in this respect, and declared that their virtuous man could never be discharged from the duty of labouring for the public good; the Epicureans, on the other hand, taught that the wise man would abstain from public affairs. It was generally supposed, however, that the ancient philosophers had on the whole recommended a life of retirement;[8] this was partly because nearly all the ancient philoso- /304/ phers agreed that, although the active life might be necessary and expedient, the life of contemplation was better and higher, and partly because the eclectic Seneca, whose influence during the Middle Ages and the Renaissance was immense, had, though he professed himself a Stoic, nevertheless declared that, when the state was past cure, the wise man might retire into solitude and work for posterity.

This debate had been continued, though in a somewhat different form, by the Fathers of the Christian Church and by the Schoolmen in their attempts to decide upon the true place of hermitism and monasticism in the life of the Church. The view which finally prevailed was that which had been expressed at the beginning by St Augustine and St Gregory and which was subsequently elaborated by Aquinas: namely, that although the contemplative life was in a sense higher, as being more like the life to come, it was nevertheless

---

8 This, certainly, was the opinion of Sir William Temple in his essay *Upon the Gardens of* Epicurus; *or, of Gardening.* Temple's essay, it is true, was written, as the title informs us, 'In the Year 1685', more than thirty years later than Marvell's poem; nevertheless, we may perhaps assume that Temple's knowledge of ancient literature and philosophy was very much what Marvell's had been when he wrote his paradoxical praise of solitude in *The Garden.* After praising Horace for refusing to become Secretary to Augustus, Temple continued (*Works,* 1720, I 175) :

But all the different Sects of Philosophers seem to have agreed in the Opinion of a Wise Man's abstaining from Publick Affairs, which is thought the Meaning of *Pythagoras's* Precept, *abstain from Beans,* by which the Affairs or Publick Resolutions in *Athens* were managed. They thought that sort of Business too gross and material for the abstracted Fineness of their Speculations . . . But above all, they esteemed Publick Business the most contrary of all others to that Tranquillity of Mind, which they esteemed and taught to be the only true Felicity of Man.

For this reason *Epicurus* passed his Life wholly in his Garden; there he Studied, there he Exercised, there he Taught his Philosophy; and indeed, no other sort of Abode seems to contribute so much, to both the Tranquillity of Mind, and Indolence of Body, which he made his Chief End. The Sweetness of Air, the Pleasantness of Smells, the Verdure of Plants, the Cleanness and Lightness of Food, the Exercises of Working or Walking; but above all, the Exemption from Cares and Solicitude, seem equally to favour and improve both Contemplation and Health, the Enjoyment of Sense and Imagination, and thereby the Quiet and Ease both of the Body and Mind.

optional, was not a life which all Christians were called upon to lead, and must at least be preceded by the active life.

Since every scholar must have been familiar with this age-long debate, it is perhaps a little remarkable that among the numerous collections of paradoxes, both in prose and verse, that were published during the sixteenth and seventeenth centuries the theme of Solitude *versus* Society or the contemplative *versus* the active life, does not seem to appear. For had it not been almost thrust upon the notice of Renaissance scholars by Petrarch's *De Vita Solitaria*, the longest and most elaborate of all celebrations of the life of retirement, contemplation and study? And Petrarch, though he continually appeals to Christian precedent and often expresses specifically Christian beliefs and ideals, is writing primarily as a scholar and humanist, and might have been expected to engage the attention of later scholars and humanists more closely than seems to have been the case. Petrarch refers several times to St Ambrose, in one of whose letters (no. XLIX), written in A.D. 390 to Sabinus, Bishop of Placenza, a letter from which Petrarch quotes, there are some remarks about the baneful impingement of Eve upon Adam's solitude which might surely have been expected, sooner or later, to provide some Italian writer of *Capitoli* or some English 'metaphysical' /305/ poet with a topic for slightly irreverent wit. Mary, declares St Ambrose, was alone when the Angel addressed her, alone when the Holy Ghost came upon her, alone when she conceived Christ.

> Peter was alone when the mystery of the sanctification of the Gentiles all over the world was made known to him. Adam was alone, and he fell not, because his mind adhered to God. But when the woman was joined to him he lost his power of abiding by the celestial precepts, and therefore he hid himself when God walked in Paradise ... From whence it appears that it is when alone that we offer ourselves to God, that we open to Him our souls, that we put off the cloak of fraud. Adam was alone when placed in Paradise; alone also when made in the image of God: but when cast out of Paradise he was not alone. The Lord Jesus was alone when he redeemed the world; for it was no herald or messenger, but the Lord Himself Who redeemed His people, although He, in Whom the Father always dwells, can never be alone. Let us also then be alone, that the Lord may be with us.[9]

I do not know whether St Ambrose was the first theologian to declare so explicitly that Adam lost his sanctity with his solitude, nor do I

---

[9] *The Letters of S. Ambrose*, in *A Library of Fathers*, Oxford 1881, pp. 317–18.

know whether the topic was treated with any significant emphasis
by his successors. Donne, whom it would not have been surprising to
find treating the topic with irreverent wit in the days of his youth,
treated it very much in the manner St Ambrose (though he does
not refer to him) in the second of the two parts into which he later
divided the sermon preached at the Hague in December 1619 on the
calling of Simon and Andrew. Donne begins this second part with a
consideration of Christ's words 'Follow me', which leads him to speak
of the virtue of humility and the sin of pride, which, he declares,
began with company and with Eve:

> Comparatively *Adam* was better then all the world beside, and yet we
> finde no act of pride in *Adam*, when he was alone. Solitude is not the
> scene of Pride; the danger of pride is in company, when we meet to
> looke upon another. But in *Adams* wife, *Eve*, her first act (that is noted)
> was an act of Pride, a hearkening to that voyce of the Serpent, *Ye shall
> be as Gods*. As soon as there were two, there was pride.[10] /306/

No doubt many other preachers and theologians, besides Donne,
had repeated these reflections which St Ambrose may or may not
have been the first to express. Sooner or later, however, it was surely
inevitable that these or similar reflections should lead some medieval
clerk or some sixteenth- or seventeenth-century wit to remark that,
as soon as Eve was joined to Adam, the serpent made up three. Never-
theless, this surely inevitable witticism, whether or no it had
occurred to anyone before, does not seem to have found its way into
print until 1668, in the seventh stanza of that charming poem be-
ginning 'Hail, old *Patrician* Trees' in Cowley's essay *Of Solitude*:

> Oh Solitude, first state of Human-kind!
>   Which blest remain'd till Man did find
>   Even his own helpers Companie.
> As soon as two (Alas) together joyn'd,
>   The Serpent made up Three.[11]

---

[10] *Sermons,* ed. Potter and Simpson, II 295, ll. 282 ff.

[11] *Works,* 1684, Qqq3ᵛ (p. 94). Cowley, it is true (and, for that matter, Marvell),
had been somewhat fumblingly and unmemorably anticipated by William Habing-
ton in his poem *To Zephirus,* whom he begs to waft himself and Castara to some
beautiful and uninhabited coast:

> Thus Paradise did our first Parents Wooe,
> To harmeless sweets, at first possesst by two.
> And o're this second, weele usurpe the throne;
> *Castara* weele obey and rule alone.

Were it not for the fact that the *Several Discourses by way of Essays, in Verse and Prose* did not appear in print until the 1668 edition of Cowley's *Works*, one might have been tempted to suppose that this stanza had been the starting-point, the initial inspiration of Marvell's *Garden*, just as two stanzas from poems in Cowley's *The Mistress* had almost certainly provided the initial inspiration for *The Definition of Love* and *To his Coy Mistress*. /307/

> Such was that happy Garden-state,
> While Man there walk'd without a Mate:
> After a Place so pure, and sweet,
> What other Help could yet be meet!
> But 'twas beyond a Mortal's share
> To wander solitary there:
> Two Paradises 'twere in one
> To live in Paradise alone.

Although this piece of wit does not seem to have been suggested to Marvell by any previous *poet*, he is here treating with a slightly irreverent wit, with, one might even say, a certain waggishness, what may well have been almost a theological commonplace, treating it with a kind of wit (hyperbolical, paradoxical, surprising, slightly shocking) not dissimilar from that which Donne had applied to more scholastic concepts—as when, for example, he declared that his mistress possessed the more than angelic power of reading thoughts directly, or that the Countess of Bedford was a divinity, to be apprehended partly by reason and partly by faith. During the seventeenth century such theological wit was often indulged in even by the gravest and most orthodox—partly, perhaps, because so much of their reading and thinking was theological, and partly because they were speaking to or writing for persons whom they could depend upon to take what they said exactly as they meant it. No one, for example, would ever have accused King James of insufficient respect for what

---

For the rich vertue of this soyle I feare,
Would be depraved, should but a third be there.

(*Poems*, ed. Allott, p. 58. The poem was first printed in Habington's *Castara*, 1634.) It is only because of the faint gleam of wit in the last line that one can speak of anticipation, for Habington, although he is being hyperbolical, is being no more paradoxical than Spenser or Milton or any sixteenth- or seventeenth-century imaginer of a Golden Age. 'Should but a third be there': it is, I suppose not impossible that this may have suggested to Cowley the paradoxical witticism that, if a second was there, a third was bound to follow, and that this third would be no other than the serpent.

he and his contemporaries regarded as the Word of God; yet King James, according to Arch-deacon Plume, once declared that 'Dr Donns verses were like yᵉ peace of God, they passed all understanding'.[12] Only those who are very secure in their faith can afford to jest about it, as Chaucer could afford to jest about Courtly Love and about learning and about much else that he held dear—a fact which, as C. S. Lewis observed, has led many modern readers to suppose that he was what the French call *un vrai business man* and that his spokesman in the *Parlement of Foules* is the Duck. Modern readers, rooted in a totalitarian, or increasingly totalitarian, society and no longer habitually aware of any distinction between things temporal and things eternal, either do not realise, or too often forget, how wide an area of play, of *Spielraum*, our older writers, especially those of the seventeenth century, were able to /308/ permit themselves. This is especially true of poets such as Donne and Marvell, who wrote their poems, not for the world at large, but for circulation among friends, whom they could depend upon to make all necessary qualifications and allowances and to admire the art and the wit. The last-quoted stanza should alone be sufficient to prevent us from taking Marvell's *Garden* too seriously, from supposing that Marvell regarded it as a full and sufficient expression of his then attitude to the relation between the contemplative and the active life—or, for that matter, to female society! His position and attitude is much more like that of a defendant or respondent in some academic debate, saying, with all the wit and eloquence at his command, all he can find to say for or against the position he has been selected to defend or to oppose.

Nevertheless, although in this poem Marvell is being deliberately paradoxical and hyperbolical, he is not being so in the riotous and almost burlesque manner of many of the Italian *Capitoli*, or many of the paradoxes in the prose collections, of some of Donne's Elegies and *Songs and Sonets*, or of his own *Character of Holland*. Marvell's paradox (his central paradox, as distinct from such a subsidiary paradox as that trees are more desire-exciting than women), that the contemplative life is superior to an active life because more like that of the unfallen Adam, is not really in *pari materia* with Donne's paradox that it is better to marry an old and ugly woman than a young and handsome one because the former's face can never change for the worse. The paradox which Marvell, with such an exquisite mingling of seriousness and light-heartedness, is here maintaining is the great, the eternal, paradox of which Aristotle was aware when

---

[12] In a notebook in the Plume Library at Maldon, MS 30, folio 17 verso: see a letter from Percy Simpson *TLS*, 25, October 1941.

he recognised that θεωρία, the life of pure contemplation, although often incompatible with the exercise of those faculties and the performance of those duties which are necessary for the preservation of human society, was nevertheless the most divine kind of life and that, in spite of those who tell us to be content to think mortal thoughts and to leave immortal thoughts to the gods, we should strive so far as possible to make ourselves immortal (ἐφ' ὅσον ἐνδέχεται ἀθανατίζειν) by living in and through the exercise of that intellect (νοῦς) which is the most potent element within us and which, small though it be, 'in power and dignity far surpasses all the rest';[13] the paradox of which Aquinas was aware when, elaborating upon Aristotle, he declared that, although the *vita contemplativa* was *non proprie humana sed superhumana*, it was nevertheless the noblest kind of life because it /309/ contained some pledge and foretaste of that immortal felicity which man was promised.

Marvell's poem may perhaps best be regarded as a graceful tribute, more substantial and serious than two stanzas in *Appleton House* with which it has some affinity, to his patron the Lord General Fairfax, who had for a time, but only for a time, exchanged a life of action for one of retirement and contemplation. In *Appleton House*, after the beautiful passage about 'the Garden of the World' that had been wasted by civil war, Marvell had reflected that there walked in the garden of Nunappleton one who, had it pleased God and himself, might have made the Garden of England flourish like his own:

> But he preferr'd to the *Cinque Ports*[14]
> These five imaginary Forts:
> And, in those half-dry Trenches, spann'd
> Pow'r which the Ocean might command.
>
> For he did, with his utmost Skill,
> *Ambition* weed, but *Conscience* till.

---

[13] *Nicomachean Ethics*, X vii (1177[b]).

[14] H. M. Margoliouth and Hugh Macdonald, in their notes on this passage, declare that Fairfax was never Lord Warden of the Cinque Ports, and assume that the allusion to the Cinque Ports was quite arbitrarily introduced to match the 'five imaginary Forts'; but, as Mrs E. E. Duncan-Jones has pointed out in a letter to *TLS* (11 November 1955), 'all powers appertaining to the Lord High Admirall of England and Lord Warden of the Cinque Ports' had, in February 1650, been assigned to the Council of State, of which Fairfax was a member, and whose meetings he continued to attend until he resigned his commission in the following June. Marvell, therefore, is alluding to the *share* which Fairfax had had in the powers of Lord Warden of the Cinque Ports, and also, as Mrs Duncan-Jones has further pointed out, in the powers ('Pow'r which the Ocean might command') of Lord High Admiral.

> *Conscience*, that Heaven-nursed Plant,
> Which most our Earthly Gardens want.
>
> (sts. XLIV–V)

In *The Garden*, we may say, Marvell has written a more sustained and unqualified panegyric upon the life Fairfax had chosen, although he, like his patron, was well aware that the active life too had its place and its necessity. For that the Lord General, although he delighted in his solitude and retirment, did not regard it as more than temporary, is a fact of which we are reminded by the words of his cousin, Brian Fairfax, in the Dedicatory Epistle to his posthumously published edition of the Lord General's *Short Memorials*: /310/

> The retired part of his Life gave him greater Satisfaction than all his former Victories, when he lived quietly in his own House at *Nun-Appleton* in *Yorkshire*; always earnestly wishing and praying for the Restitution of the Royal Family, and fully resolved to lay hold on the first Good Opportunity to contribute his part towards it; which made him always lookt upon with a jealous eye by the Usurpers of that time.[15]

Some time after the death of his famous cousin (who was considerably older than himself) Brian Fairfax had celebrated this retired life at Nunappleton (recalling, it may well be, the post-Restoration years as well as the 1650's) in a poem entitled *The Vocal Oak. Upon the cutting down of the woods at Nun-Appleton.* After alluding (like Marvell in *Appleton House*) to the days when Nunappleton was a nunnery and declaring that it could tell many 'pretty stories' of the 'vestal virgins', and after recalling, in a passage reminiscent of Marvell's poem *Upon the Hill and Grove at Bill-borow*, how the Lord General had preserved its companions from the axe, the oak speaks of its great master's delight in 'this pleasant place':

> Where twenty years' retirement pleased him more
> Than all the trophies he had won before.
> Oft would he bring a book, and sit him down,
> Less glorious in arms than in his gown;
> All ages past, and persons that are gone,
> Were not, to me who saw them, better known.
> He read diviner things than Druids knew,
> Such mysteries were then revealed to few;
> For his chief study was God's sacred law,

---

15 *Short Memorials of Thomas Lord Fairfax. Written by Himself.* 1699, p. vii.

> And all his life did comments on it draw.
> As Israel's king at last lay by his sword,
> And took the sacred harp to praise his Lord,
> Like some religious hermit now he seem'd,
> By all the world (least by himself) esteem'd,
> Fain would I hear him tell what he had done—
> How many battles fought, as many won;
> When all the fields and villages around
> Heard his victorious drums and trumpets sound;
> When all these woods did echo forth his praise,
> And wish'd, t'adorn his head, we'd all been bays.[16]

/311/ I return to what I have called that central and eternal para-
dox which Aristotle first clearly formulated and which Aquinas Chris-
tianised. Man is both human and divine, or potentially divine;
although, as human, he must attend to 'his station and its duties', he
must also, as potentially divine, cherish so far as possible the divine
spark within himself and recognise, even if he cannot always pursue
it, that the life of contemplation is higher and better than the life of
action. The life of contemplation is indeed the final justification of
the life of action, since as Aristotle said, we are only unleisurely in
order that we may be at leisure (ἀσχολούμεθα γὰρ ἵνα σχολάξωμεν), un-
derstanding leisure, σχολή, not as mere relaxation but as a kind of
festival or celebration in which we may achieve what the Shorter
Catechism describes as man's chief end, namely, to glorify God and
to enjoy him for ever. It is this central and eternal paradox that seems
to have been revealed with fresh force and clarity to all who knew
him by the life of the Lord General Fairfax. No man, when he rec-
ognised its authority, responded with more alacrity to the call of
action; no man, when the time for action had passed or had been
suspended, recognised more clearly the essential superiority of the
life of contemplation, or embraced it more wholeheartedly and
happily. It was in this man's society, and, as I cannot but think,
chiefly for him, that Marvell wrote his panegyric on solitude and
contemplation in *The Garden*: seriously, because the life of contem-
plation was divine; delightedly and delightfully, because it was the
highest delight of which man was capable; and yet, at the same time,
light-heartedly (with witty allusions to the metamorphoses of Daphne
and Syrinx and to the banefulness of Eve), because, for such a
being as man in such a world as the present one, the life of con-

---

[16] This, together with some other poems by Brian Fairfax, will be found on
pp. cxxi–v of G. W. Johnson's *Memoirs of the Reign of Charles I*, 1848, vol. I.

templation could seldom be more than an interlude and might at
any time be interrupted by the claims, ultimately and eternally
lower, immediately and temporally higher, of action. Is not, perhaps,
the vibration and the iridescence, the delightedness and the delight-
fulness, which interpenetrates so many of these poems which, as I
think, Marvell wrote during his two years' sojourn at Nunappleton—
their continuous vibration, as distinct from that forgetful and ex-
clusive luxuriance in a particular mood which characterises so much
romantic poetry, between seriousness and light-heartedness (as an
electric spark vibrates between the positively and negatively charged
terminals of an induction coil)—is not this, perhaps, a reflection of
Marvell's continuous awareness of what I have called the 'Paradox',
of his awareness that what he was enjoying, though indeed a fore-
taste of man's highest felicity, was but a temporarily /312/ conceded
joy? Even as the society and the civilisation in and out of which they
were written, and of which to many they have seemed the most gra-
cious flower, itself existed but for a season and a time—as a sugges-
tion, perhaps, of something that might be.

Questions

In style as well as content the selection from the late J. B. Leishman's
book *The Art of Marvell's Poetry* is an appropriate conclusion for this
handbook of critical essays. Leishman is reflective, appreciative, and system-
atic. While he is clearly aware of the difficulties critics have encountered
with "The Garden," and the battles which have been fought over the poem,
he is in most respects detached from such activity. He has the ability to
accept and reject the views of others (see discussion of Kermode's essay,
p. 293) at the same time. Without being permissive, his essay demonstrates
a tolerance of the "to each his own" tendencies of new criticism as well as a
respect for those of a more historical conscience. Leishman, once again,
serves us as a guide through the Garden. We get the impression that he may
have lived there too.

Do you find Mr. Leishman's prose versions and lists of themes a help
or a hindrance to your appreciation of the poem?

Is Leishman's concentration on the "dialectical and pictorial" and the
themes of solitude and contemplation more or less effective than other
critics' attempts to deal with the vexed points in the poem?

How does Leishman's classification of "The Garden" as a cross between
two types, the "Reply" and the "Paradox," modify your understanding

of genre? How many literary subdivisions do you now think qualify to be considered as generic? What historical tests might you apply in solving this problem?

Mr. Leishman is the only critic to give detailed attention to the tone of Marvell's poem. How could this serve as a useful corrective to some of the other interpretations in this book?

Suggestions for Papers

As the concept of genre implies historical continuity, so there is a continuity established with the criticism on "The Garden" from Empson to Leishman. After Empson, everyone realizes the necessity of reading the poem as a whole, though this does not mean that all do so. All of the critics are concerned with a context for the garden, whether this context be historical or not. A language for criticism is clearly apparent, with key terms such as genre, paradox, libertine, image, symbol, expression, Neo-Platonic, Hermetic, Epicurean. Literary historians provide us with terms like the first three in this list. The second three terms belong to the New Critics' intrinsic approach to literature. "Neo-Platonic, Hermetic, Epicurean" are terms typical of the language used by historians of ideas, in literature or in general. You may decide to apply your talents according to these "norms," or not, but you ought to have at least some practical experience with the disciplines represented by the three major schools of modern criticism demonstrated in this collection.

Exercise:

Write a complete paraphrase, or "parody," of "The Garden," using as few of Marvell's own words as possible. What kind of language does the poem suggest to you?

Exercise:

Many of the critics use a stanza-by-stanza reading of "The Garden" as a structural outline for their essay. Write a brief line-by-line explanation of the poem. Keep in mind that your explanation ought to resemble a logical, or at least a consistent argument. When you are finished, notice which stanzas required more explaining, or suggested more alternatives, than others. Have you been fair to the sense of the poem as a whole?

Literary history combines the principle of intrinsic analysis with a study of poetry according to its type, or genre. With more sophistication and a wide selection of material to examine, the literary historian may begin to outline and describe broader trends in literary style such as the metaphysical or Jonsonian schools already mentioned. Biography is sometimes important, as in the relationship between Marvell and Fairfax, but this is really another matter.

Research Exercise:

Using the introduction and the essays in this collection for suggestions and documentation, describe as best you can the genre to which "The Garden" belongs. Remember Pierre Legouis' warning that it is necessary to verify, historically, the existence and relative importance of genre. Since the critics do not always agree on what kind of poem "The Garden" is, you will have to defend your description against those whose opinion you have rejected.

Consider the matter of biography. Have the critics in this collection convinced you that the details of Marvell's life at Fairfax's Yorkshire estate are essential for an accurate and complete understanding of "The Garden"? How influential were Marvell's "cavalier" acquaintances in London? The defense or rejection of biography as an appropriate concern of the literary critic is a worthwhile essay topic. But additional research must be done, beginning with the biographical texts listed in the bibliography.

As the literary historian is primarily concerned with matters of style and form, the study of ideas in literature emphasizes the content or meaning of a poem. But since the meaning of a poem can only be discovered through its literary forms—images, symbols—some degree of intrinsic analysis is necessary in this method of criticism. The literary historian verifies his conclusions with the physical evidence of poems and other documents. The historian of ideas directs his attention to the language of poetry and establishes, by interpretive argument and citation of parallel texts using the same or similar language, a set of meanings which successfully explain a particular passage, stanza, and then the whole poem.

Research Exercise:

Write a limited thematic analysis of "The Garden," in the manner of an intellectual historian. Give a complete reading of the lines

> Annihilating all that's made
> To a green Thought in a green Shade.

Use as much information supplied by the critics as possible. Does your reading need to be modified in any way, so as not to distort the sense of the complete poem?

Research Essay:

General guidelines for a complete research essay are printed at the beginning of this book. Topics may be chosen from the questions following each critical essay. We suggest that you consider carefully not only the topic but the method you will use to determine the nature of the evidence needed, to explore ideas and to prove your point.

Additional Readings

I. Editions of Marvell

The Complete Works in Verse and Prose of Andrew Marvell. Edited by
A. B. Grosart. 3 vols. London, 1873.
The Poems and Letters. Edited by H. M. Margoliouth. 2 vols. Oxford:
Clarendon Press, 1963.
The Latin Poetry of Andrew Marvell. Translated and annotated by William
A. McQueen and Kiffin A. Rockwell. Chapel Hill: University of North
Carolina Press, 1964.

II. Biography

Aubrey, John. *Brief Lives.* Edited by Oliver Lawson Dick. Ann Arbor:
University of Michigan Press, 1962.
Legouis, Pierre. *Andrew Marvell: Poet, Puritan, Patriot.* Oxford: Clarendon
Press, 1965.
————. *Andre Marvell: Poete, Puritain, Patriote.* Paris: H. Didier, 1928.
Wallace, John M. *Destiny his Choice: The Loyalism of Andrew Marvell.*
Cambridge: Cambridge University Press, 1968.

III. Secondary Sources

Bain, Carl E. "The Latin Poetry of Andrew Marvell," *Philological Quarterly,*
XXXVIII (October, 1959), 436-49.
Berger, Harry, Jr. "Marvell's 'Garden': Still Another Interpretation," *Modern Language Quarterly,* 28 (September, 1967), 285-304.
Berthoff, Ann E. *The Resolved Soul; A Study of Marvell's Major Poems.*
Princeton: Princeton University Press, 1970.
Birrell, Augustine. *Andrew Marvell.* New York: Macmillan Co., 1905.
Bradbrook, F. W. "The Poetry of Andrew Marvell," in *From Donne to
Marvell.* Edited by Boris Ford. London: Penguin Books, 1956, pp.
193-204.
Bradbrook, M. C. and Thomas, M. G. Lloyd. *Andrew Marvell.* Cambridge:
University Press, 1961.
Brooks, Cleanth. "Literary Criticism," *English Institute Essays,* 1946 (New
York, 1947), 127-58.

Chambers, A. B. " 'I Was But an Inverted Tree': Notes toward the History of an Idea," *Studies in the Renaissance,* VIII (1961), 291-99.

Colie, Rosalie L. *My Echoing Song: Andrew Marvell's Poetry of Criticism.* Princeton: Princeton University Press, 1970.

Davison, Dennis. "Notes on Marvell's 'The Garden'," *Notes and Queries,* XIII (January, 1966), 25-26.

Hartman, Geoffrey H. "Marvell, St. Paul, and the Body of Hope," *English Literary History,* XXXI (June, 1964), 175-94.

Hecht, Anthony. "Shades of Keats and Marvell," *The Hudson Review,* XV (Spring 1962), 50-71.

Hyman, Lawrence William. "Marvell's Garden," *English Literary History,* XXV (March, 1958), 13-22.

————. *Andrew Marvell.* New York: Grosset & Dunlap, 1964.

King, A. H. "Some Notes on Andrew Marvell's 'Garden'," *English Studies,* XX (June, 1938), 118-21.

McQueen, William A. "The Missing Stanzas in Marvell's 'Hortus'," *Philological Quarterly,* XLIV (April, 1965), 173-79.

Poggioli, Rennato. "The Pastoral of the Self," *Daedalus,* LXXXVIII (Fall 1959), 686-99.

Press, John. *Andrew Marvell.* London: Published for the British Council and the National Book League by Longmans, Green, 1958.

Sackville-West, Victoria Mary. *Andrew Marvell.* London: Faber & Faber Ltd., 1929.

Smith, Harold Wendell. "Cowley, Marvell and the Second Temple," *Scrutiny,* XIX (Spring 1953), 184-205.

Stempel, Daniel. " 'The Garden': Marvell's Cartesian Ecstasy," *Journal of the History of Ideas,* 28 (January-March, 1967), 99-114.

Toliver, Harold E. *Marvell's Ironic Vision.* New Haven: Yale University Press, 1965.

Walcutt, Charles C. "Marvell's 'The Garden,' 46-48," *Explicator,* XXIV (January, 1966), Item 48.

Williamson, George. "The Context of Marvell's 'Hortus' and 'Garden'," *Modern Language Notes,* LXXVI (November, 1961), 590-98.

General Instructions
for a Research Paper

If your instructor gives you any specific directions about the format of your research paper that differ from the directions given here, you are, of course, to follow his directions. Otherwise, you can observe these directions with the confidence that they represent fairly standard conventions.

A research paper represents a student's synthesis of his reading in a number of primary and secondary works, with an indication, in footnotes, of the source of quotations used in the paper or of facts cited in paraphrased material. A *primary* source is the text of a work as it issued from the pen of the author or some document contemporary with the work. The following, for instance, would be considered primary sources: a manuscript copy of the work; first editions of the work and any subsequent editions authorized by the writer; a modern scholarly edition of the text; an author's comment about his work in letters, memoirs, diaries, journals, or periodicals; published comments on the work by the author's contemporaries. A *secondary* source would be any interpretation, explication, or evaluation of the work printed, usually several years after the author's death, in critical articles and books, in literary histories, and in biographies of the author. In this casebook, the text of the work, any variant versions of it, any commentary on the work by the author himself or his contemporaries may be considered as primary sources; the editor's Introduction, the articles from journals, and the excerpts from books are to be considered secondary sources. The paper that you eventually write will become a secondary source.

Plagiarism

The cardinal sin in the academic community is plagiarism. The rankest form of plagiarism is the verbatim reproduction of someone else's words without any indication that the passage is a quotation. A lesser but still serious form of plagiarism is to report, in your own words, the fruits of someone else's research without acknowledging the source of your information or interpretation.

You can take this as an inflexible rule: every verbatim quotation in your paper must be either enclosed in quotation marks or single-spaced and inset from the left-hand margin and must be followed by a footnote number. Students who merely change a few words or phrases in a quotation and present the passage as their own work are still guilty of plagiarism. Passages of genuine paraphrase must be footnoted too if the information or idea or interpretation contained in the paraphrase cannot be presumed to be known by ordinary educated people or at least by readers who would be interested in the subject you are writing about.

The penalties for plagiarism are usually very severe. Don't run the risk of a failing grade on the paper or even of a failing grade in the course.

Lead-Ins

Provide a lead-in for all quotations. Failure to do so results in a serious breakdown in coherence. The lead-in should at least name the person who is being quoted. The ideal lead-in, however, is one that not only names the person but indicates the pertinence of the quotation.

Examples:

(typical lead-in for a single-spaced, inset quotation)

```
Irving Babbitt makes this observation about
Flaubert's attitude toward women:
```

(typical lead-in for quotation worked into the frame of one's sentence)

```
Thus the poet sets out to show how the present
age, as George Anderson puts it, "negates the
values of the earlier revolution."[7]
```

Full Names

The first time you mention anyone in a paper give the full name of the person. Subsequently you may refer to him by his last name.

Examples:
```
First allusion—Ronald S. Crane
Subsequent allusions—Professor Crane,
as Crane says.
```

Ellipses

Lacunae in a direct quotation are indicated with *three spaced periods,* in addition to whatever punctuation mark was in the text at the point where you truncated the quotation. *Hit the space-bar of your typewriter between each period.* Usually there is no need to put the ellipsis-periods at the beginning or the end of a quotation.

Example: "The poets were not striving to communicate with their audience; . . . By and large, the Romantics were seeking . . . to express their unique personalities."[8]

Brackets

Brackets are used to enclose any material interpolated into a direct quotation. The abbreviation *sic,* enclosed in brackets, indicates that the error of spelling, grammar, or fact in a direct quotation has been copied as it was in the source being quoted. If your typewriter does not have special keys for brackets, draw the brackets neatly with a pen.

Examples: "He [Theodore Baum] maintained that Confucianism [the primary element in Chinese philosophy] aimed at teaching each individual to accept his lot in life."[12]

"Paul Revear [sic] made his historic ride on April 18, 1875 [sic]."[15]

Summary Footnote

A footnote number at the end of a sentence which is not enclosed in quotation marks indicates that only *that* sentence is being documented in the footnote. If you want to indicate that the footnote documents more than one sentence, put a footnote number at the end of the *first* sentence of the paraphrased passage and use some formula like this in the footnote:

[16]For the information presented in this and the following paragraph, I am indebted to Marvin Magalaner, Time of Apprenticeship: the Fiction of Young James Joyce (London, 1959), pp. 81-93.

Citing the Edition

The edition of the author's work being used in a paper should always be cited in the first footnote that documents a quotation from that work. You can obviate the need for subsequent footnotes to that edition by using some formula like this:

[4]Nathaniel Hawthorne, "Young Goodman Brown," as printed in Young Goodman Brown, ed. Thomas E.

Connolly, Charles E. Merrill Literary Casebooks
(Columbus, Ohio, 1968), pp. 3-15. This edition will
be used throughout the paper, and hereafter all
quotations from this book will be documented with a
page-number in parentheses at the end of the
quotation.

Notetaking

Although all the material you use in your paper may be contained in this
casebook, you will find it easier to organize your paper if you work from
notes written on 3 x 5 or 4 x 6 cards. Besides, you should get practice in the
kind of notetaking you will have to do for other term-papers, when you will
have to work from books and articles in, or on loan from, the library.

An ideal note is a self-contained note — one which has all the information
you would need if you used anything from that note in your paper. A note
will be self-contained if it carries the following information:

(1) The information or quotation *accurately* copied.
(2) Some system for distinguishing direct quotation from paraphrase.
(3) All the bibliographical information necessary for documenting that
    note — full name of the author, title, volume number (if any), place
    of publication, publisher, publication date, page numbers.
(4) If a question covered more than one page in the source, the note-card
    should indicate which part of the quotation occurred on one page and
    which part occurred on the next page. The easiest way to do this is
    to put the next page number in parentheses after the last word on
    one page and before the first word on the next page.

In short, your note should be so complete that you would never have to go
back to the original source to gather any piece of information about that note.

Footnote Forms

The footnote forms used here follow the conventions set forth in the
MLA Style Sheet, Revised Edition, ed. William Riley Parker, which is now
used by more than 100 journals and more than thirty university presses in
the United States. Copies of this pamphlet can be purchased for fifty cents
from your university bookstore or from the Modern Language Association,
62 Fifth Avenue, New York, New York 10011. If your teacher or your
institution prescribes a modified form of this footnoting system, you should,
of course, follow that system.

A primary footnote, the form used the first time a source is cited, supplies
four pieces of information: (1) author's name, (2) title of the source,

(3) publication information, (4) specific location in the source of the information or quotation. A secondary footnote is the shorthand form of documentation after the source has been cited in full the first time.

Your instructor may permit you to put all your footnotes on separate pages at the end of your paper. But he may want to give you practice in putting footnotes at the bottom of the page. Whether the footnotes are put at the end of the paper or at the bottom of the page, they should observe this format of spacing: (1) the first line of each footnote should be indented, usually the same number of spaces as your paragraph indentations; (2) all subsequent lines of the footnote should start at the lefthand margin; (3) there should be single-spacing within each footnote and double-spacing between each footnote.

Example:

¹⁰Ruth Wallerstein, <u>Richard</u> <u>Crashaw</u>: <u>A</u> <u>Study</u> <u>in</u> <u>Style</u> <u>and</u> <u>Poetic</u> <u>Development</u>, University of Wisconsin Studies in Language and Literature, No. 37 (Madison, 1935), p. 52.

Primary Footnotes

(The form to be used the *first* time a work is cited)

¹Paull F. Baum, <u>Ten</u> <u>Studies</u> <u>in</u> <u>the</u> <u>Poetry</u> <u>of</u> <u>Matthew</u> <u>Arnold</u> (Durham, N.C., 1958), p. 37.

    (book by a single author; p. is the abbreviation of *page*)

²René Wellek and Austin Warren, <u>Theory</u> <u>of</u> <u>Litera-</u> <u>ture</u> (New York, 1949), pp. 106-7.

    (book by two authors; pp. is the abbreviation of *pages*)

³William Hickling Prescott, <u>History</u> <u>of</u> <u>the</u> <u>Reign</u> <u>of</u> <u>Philip</u> <u>the</u> <u>Second,</u> <u>King</u> <u>of</u> <u>Spain,</u> ed. John Foster Kirk (Philadelphia, 1871), II, 47.

(an edited work of more than one volume; *ed.* is the abbreviation for "edited by"; note that whenever a volume number is cited, the abbreviation p. or pp. is *not* used in front of the page number)

⁴John Pick, ed., <u>The</u> <u>Windhover</u> (Columbus, Ohio, 1968), p. 4.

(form for quotation from an editor's Introduction — as, for instance, in this casebook series; here *ed.* is the abbreviation for "editor")

⁵A.S.P. Woodhouse, "Nature and Grace in <u>The</u> <u>Faerie</u> <u>Queen,</u>" in <u>Elizabethan</u> <u>Poetry</u>: <u>Modern</u> <u>Essays</u> <u>in</u>

<u>Criticism</u>, ed. Paul J. Alpers (New York, 1967),
pp. 346-7.

(chapter or article from an edited collection)

⁶Morton D. Paley, "Tyger of Wrath," <u>PMLA</u>, LXXXI
(December, 1966), 544.

(an article from a periodical; note that because the volume number is
cited no p. or pp. precedes the page number; the titles of periodicals are
often abbreviated in footnotes but are spelled out in the Bibliography; here,
for instance, *PMLA* is the abbreviation for *Publications of the Modern
Language Association*)

Secondary Footnotes

(Abbreviated footnote forms to be used after a work has been cited once
in full)

⁷Baum, p. 45.

(abbreviated form for work cited in footnote #1; note that the secondary
footnote is indented the same number of spaces as the first line of primary
footnotes)

⁸Wellek and Warren, pp. 239-40.

(abbreviated form for work cited in footnote #2)

⁹Prescott, II, 239.

(abbreviated form for work cited in footnote #3; because this is a
multi-volume work, the volume number must be given in addition to the
page number)

¹⁰<u>Ibid</u>., p. 245.

(refers to the immediately preceding footnote — that is, to page 245 in
the second volume of Prescott's history; *ibid.* is the abbreviation of the
Latin adverb *ibidem* meaning "in the same place"; note that this abbrevia-
tion is italicized or underlined and that it is followed by a period, because
it is an abbreviation)

¹¹<u>Ibid</u>., III, 103.

(refers to the immediately preceding footnote — that is, to Prescott's work
again; there must be added to *ibid.* only what changes from the preceding
footnote; here the volume and page changed; note that there is no p. before
103, because a volume number was cited)

¹²Baum, pp. 47-50.

(refers to the same work cited in footnote #7 and ultimately to the work
cited in full in footnote #1)

[13]Paley, p. 547.

(refers to the article cited in footnote #6)

[14]Rebecca P. Parkin, "Mythopoeic Activity in the Rape of the Lock," ELH, XXI (March, 1954), 32.

(since this article from the *Journal of English Literary History* has not been previously cited in full, it must be given in full here)

[15]Ibid., pp. 33-4.

(refers to Parkin's article in the immediately preceding footnote)

Bibliography Forms

Note carefully the differences in bibliography forms from footnote forms: (1) the last name of the author is given first, since bibliography items are arranged alphabetically according to the surname of the author (in the case of two or more authors of a work, only the name of the first author is reversed); (2) the first line of each bibliography item starts at the lefthand margin; subsequent lines are indented; (3) periods are used instead of commas, and parentheses do not enclose publication information; (4) the publisher is given in addition to the place of publication; (5) the first and last pages of articles and chapters are given; (6) most of the abbreviations used in footnotes are avoided in the Bibliography.

The items are arranged here alphabetically as they would appear in the Bibliography of your paper.

Baum, Paull F. Ten Studies in the Poetry of Matthew Arnold. Durham, N.C.: University of North Carolina Press, 1958.

Paley, Morton D. "Tyger of Wrath," Publications of the Modern Language Association, LXXXI (December, 1966), 540-51.

Parkin, Rebecca P. "Mythopoeic Activity in the Rape of the Lock," Journal of English Literary History, XXI (March, 1954), 30-8.

Pick, John, editor. The Windhover. Columbus, Ohio: Charles E. Merrill Publishing Company, 1968.

Prescott, William Hickling. History of the Reign of Philip the Second, King of Spain. Edited by John Foster Kirk. 3 volumes. Philadelphia: J.B. Lippincott and Company, 1871.

Wellek, René and Austin Warren. <u>Theory</u> <u>of</u> <u>Litera-</u>
<u>ture</u>. New York: Harcourt, Brace & World, Inc.,
1949.

Woodhouse, A.S.P. "Nature and Grace in <u>The</u> <u>Faerie</u>
<u>Queene</u>," in <u>Elizabethan</u> <u>Poetry</u>: <u>Modern</u> <u>Essays</u> <u>in</u>
<u>Criticism</u>. Edited by Paul J. Alpers. New York:
Oxford University Press, 1967, pp. 345-79.

*If the form for some work that you are using in your paper is not given
in these samples of footnote and bibliography entries, ask your instructor
for advice as to the proper form.*

Officially Withdrawn

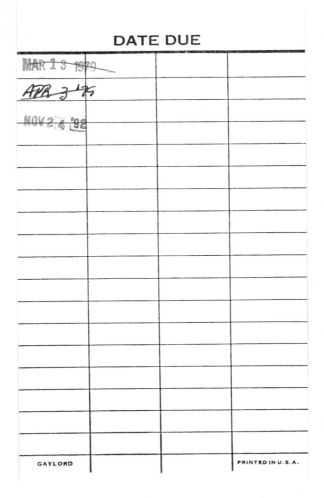